INDIAN FINANCIAL SYSTEM

INDIAN FINANCIAL SYSTEM

D.K. Murthy
Reader
Department of Commerce, Bangalore University
Bangalore, Karnataka

Venugopal
Co-ordinator for M.Com
Govt. R.C. College of Commerce & Management
Bangalore, Karnataka

TECHSAR™
NEW DELHI

Published and Printed by
TechSar Pvt. Ltd.
4435–36/7, Ansari Road, Daryaganj
New Delhi-110 002 (India)
E-mail: tech_info@techsarworld.com
Website: www.techsarworld.com

ISBN 978-81-88237-88-3

Reprint 2025

To

Dr. B.C. Sanjeevaiah

Professor and Dean, Department of Commerce
Bangalore University, Bangalore

PREFACE

It gives us immense pleasure in presenting this book before the students and teaching community. It is a humble, honest and sincere effort undertaken by us keeping in view the economic reforms. The financial system in India has undergone a change at par with international dimensions because of acceptance of the new economic reforms and particularly financial sector reforms.

The students should know how financial system has changed the face of economic development in India and how the financial institutions, instruments and markets have coped with these changes, which are the whistle blowers brought by the financial system regulators, what is the changed scenario in insurance sectors, mutual funds industry, paradigm shift in technology, work culture in banking, and also the monetary policy of the Reserve Bank of India. All this and more has been discussed in this book.

Each chapter in the book starts with learning objectives, followed by meticulous arrangement of sub-topics and at the end of each chapter objective, analytical and essay-type questions. Although, a good number of books are available on the topic, but none of them suits the specific needs of the students. After thoroughly pursuing the competing books, we have authored this book giving adequate contemporary examples appropriately. The book is the result of vast research and teaching experience. Responsibility for any errors, omissions or inadequacies rests entirely with us. Suggestions for improvements are earnestly solicited.

D.K. Murthy
Venugopal

ACKNOWLEDGEMENTS

We express our sincere gratitude to our parents, family members and friends for their encouragement and support to us. We would also like to thank Dr. B.C. Sanjeevaiah, Dean, Department of Commerce, Bangalore University, Bangalore for his help in our endeavour. Last but not the least, due acknowledgement and thanks to Dr. L.N. Sheshagiri, Senior Lecturer in English, Maharani Art, Commerce and Management College, Bangalore for his help in editing the manuscript of our book.

D.K. Murthy
Venugopal

CONTENTS

Chapter 1
FINANCIAL SYSTEM

OUTLINE

- Financial System
- Meaning
- Structure of Financial System
- Financial Institutions
    - Banking
    - Non-banking
- Financial Markets
    - Classification of financial markets
    - Money markets
    - Capital markets
    - Primary markets
    - Secondary markets
- Financial Instruments
- Financial Services
- Financial Assets
- Money Markets
- Instruments of Money Market
    - Call money market
    - Commercial bill market
    - Certificate of deposits
    - Commercial papers
    - Discount market

Question Bank
Skill Development

LEARNING OBJECTIVES

After reading the chapter you should be able to answer:

- Meaning of Indian financial system
- Components of financial system
- Differences between banking and non-banking institutions
- Classification of financial markets
- Meaning of money markets
- Characteristics
- Prerequisites
- Instruments of money market

FINANCIAL SYSTEM

Efficient and sound Financial System of a country plays an important role in the nation's economic development. The economic development of a country depends upon the savings mobilization, credit creation and the flow of these funds to the investors by raising funds through the capital market, or borrowing from financial institutions. The savings of individuals, corporate sector and government should be mobilized by the financial institutions through financial markets by creating financial instruments and claims against themselves.

The flow chart of funds from savers to borrowers is given in the Figure 1.1

The funds of savers mobilized by various financial institutions will flow to the borrowers (users) in the following way which is mentioned in detail in the Figure 1.1.

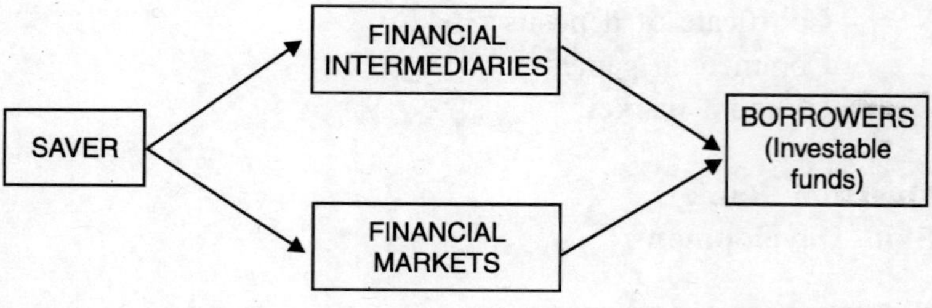

Figure 1.1 Flow of funds from savers to borrowers.

The funds borrowed by the borrowers are invested in various productive activities which in turn increase the GDP, national income, supports other sectors of an economy to increase overall development of an economy besides generating employment.

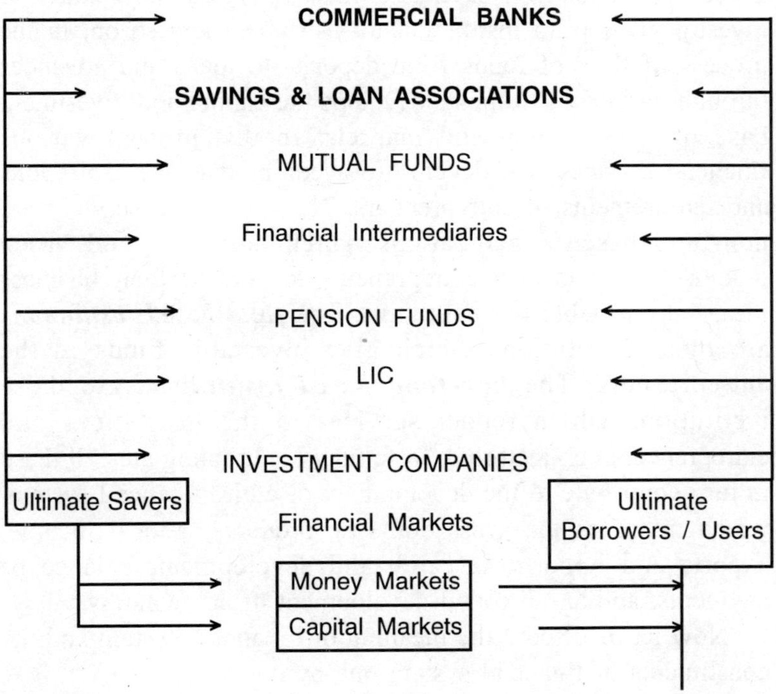

Figure 1.2. Flow of funds from savers to borrowers.

Financial system comprises financial institutions, financial markets, financial instruments, financial services and financial assets. A well developed country will have well organized financial institutions which mobilize savings from sectors like household, business and government. They channelize these savings (funds) collected in the form of deposits and also credit created by these institutions to different sectors of an economy like industry, agriculture, services in the form of loans and advances. In the process of deposit mobilization and advancing loans the financial system introduces various instruments. The development of more number of instruments for deposit raising and advances is a symptom of development of an economy. It demands well developed financial markets of both primary and secondary or money market and capital markets for converting the financial instruments into liquidity. This increases the flow of funds from savings to investment, or from lending to investment or from instrument to instrument and so on. In the process of flow of funds from deposits to loans and advances through various instruments develops the capital and investment base of an economy and markets. In this process various financial services will develop to accommodate the aspirations and requirements of entrepreneurs. These financial services are non-fund based organizations which help the fund based organizations and also entrepreneurs to convert their business ideas into a viable business units. The ***fund based institutions*** are those institutions which give investable funds to the entrepreneurs. The ***non-fund based institutions*** are those institutions which render services to the institutions and entrepreneurs i.e., factoring, forfeiting, credit rating etc. All these in turn contribute to the development of entire financial system, which improves the gross domestic product, national income, exports and imports, research and development, balance of payments, and an all round development of an economy.

Now let us discuss the meaning of Financial System and the constituents of financial system one by one.

MEANING OF FINANCIAL SYSTEM

Financial system is ***a set of complex and closely connected or interlinked financial institutions, or organized and unorganized financial markets, financial instruments and services which facilitate the transfer of funds.***

It means that the financial system has a number of complex and closely connected or interlinked institutions like banking institutions: public, private, new generation banks, foreign banks, co-operative banks, RRBs, besides many non-banking financial institutions like LIC, GIC, mutual funds, investment trusts, finance corporations, finance companies which are complex to classify but interrelated. Similarly the financial markets are also for movement of funds from savers to intermediaries and from intermediaries to investors. In the meanwhile they are also assisted by financial services like leasing, factoring, credit rating etc. All these will help the transfer of funds in an economy from savers to investors.

STRUCTURE OF FINANCIAL SYSTEM

The financial structure refers to ***shape, constituents and their order in the financial system.*** The financial system consists of specialized and unspecialized financial institutions, organized and unorganized financial markets, financial instruments and services which facilitate transfer of funds.

A financial system consists of financial institutions, financial markets, financial instruments and financial services which are all regulated by ***regulators like Ministry of Finance, the Company Law Board, RBI, SEBI, IRDA, Department of Economic Affairs, Department of Company Affairs, etc.,*** which facilitate the process of smooth and efficient transfer of funds.

Now let us understand the structure of Indian financial system through Figure 1.3.

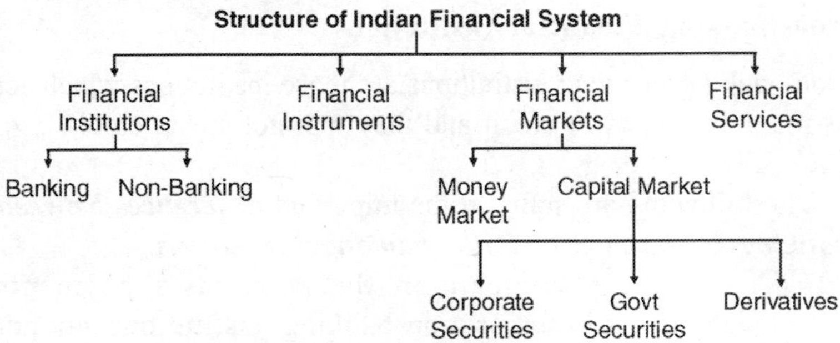

Figure 1.3. Structure of Indian Financial System

Let us discuss each element of financial system to understand its significance in the economy. The financial institutions may be business organizations or non-business organizations.

FINANCIAL INSTITUTIONS

Financial institutions are the business organizations that act as mobilisers of savings, and as purveyors of credit or finance. They also provide various financial services to the community. These financial business organisations ***deal in financial assets such as deposits, loans, securities, and so on.*** These assets can be seen on the asset side of the balance sheet of banks or any other financial institutions.

The **non-financial institutions** are ***those business organisations, which deal in real assets such as machinery, equipment, stocks of goods***, ***real assets*** etc. These assets can be seen on the asset side of the balance sheet of the manufacturing companies.

The financial institutions are classified into banking institutions and non-banking institutions.

Banking Financial Institutions

Banking institutions are those institutions, which participate in the economy's payments system, i.e., they provide transaction services. Their deposits liabilities constitute a major part of the national money supply and they can, as a whole, create deposits or credit, which is money.

Non-Banking Financial Institutions

Non-banking financial institutions are those institutions which act as mere purveyors of credit and they will not create credit. e.g., LIC, UTI, IDBI.

The following are some of the important ***differences between banking institutions and non-banking institutions***.

1. The banks participate in the economy's payments mechanism. Whereas non-banking institutions do not participate in the payments mechanism of an economy.
2. Banks provide transaction services like providing overdraft facility, issue of cheque books, traveller's cheque, demand

draft, transfer of funds etc., whereas the non-banking institutions do not provide any transaction services.

3. Bank deposits (are the liabilities to the banks) constitute a major part of the national money supply. Whereas the money supply of the non-banking institutions is small.
4. Banks create credit. It is one of the main functions of the banks. But non-banking institutions do not create credit.
5. Banks are subjected to fulfilment of some legal requirements like CRR, Capital Adequacy Ratio (CAR). Whereas the non-banking institutions are not subjected to these legal requirements.
6. Banks can advance credit by creating claims against themselves. Whereas the non-banking institutions cannot do so.

According to **Sayers** banking institutions are '***creators***' of credit and NBFIs are mere '***purveyors***' of credit.

The financial institutions are also classified into financial intermediaries and non-financial intermediaries.

Financial Intermediaries

Financial intermediaries are those institutions which intermediate between savers and investors; they lend money as well as mobilize savings; their liabilities are towards the ultimate savers, while their assets are from the investors or borrowers.

Non-Financial Intermediaries

Non-intermediaries are those institutions which do the loan business but their resources are not directly obtained from the savers. Many non-banking institutions also act as intermediaries and when they do so they are known as non-banking financial intermediaries e.g., LIC, GIC, IDBI, IFC, NABARD.

Another part of the financial system is Financial Markets.

FINANCIAL MARKETS

Efficient financial markets are a *sine qua non* for speedy economic development. The vibrant financial market enhances the efficiency of capital formation. This market facilitates the flow of savings into investment against capital formation. The role of financial markets in the financial system is quite unique. The financial markets bridge one set of financial intermediaries with another set of players.

Financial markets are ***the centres or arrangements that provide facilities for buying and selling of financial claims and services.*** The participants in the financial markets are corporations, financial institutions, individuals and the government. These participants trade in financial products in these markets. They trade either directly or through brokers and dealers in organized exchanges or off-exchanges. They are classified into money market and capital market, primary markets and secondary markets, organized markets and unorganized markets, etc.

Classification of Financial Markets

There are different ways of classifying financial markets. One way of classifying the financial markets is by the type of financial claim into the debt market and the equity market. The debt market is the financial market for fixed claims like debt instruments. The equity market is the financial market for residual claims i.e., equity instruments

A second way of classifying the financial markets into money market and capital market is on the basis of maturity of claims.

Money Markets

A market where short-term funds are borrowed and lent is called 'money market'. Money markets deal in the short-term assets (with a period of maturity of one year or less), which are near substitutes for money. Examples of money market are treasury bills market, call money market, commercial bills market, commercial paper, certificate of deposits, Repurchase Options (REPOs), Inter-Bank Participation Certificates (IBPCs), Securitised debt, Options, Financial Futures, Forward Rate Agreements, Swaps, etc.

Capital Markets

Capital markets deal in the long-term claims, securities, and stocks with a maturity period of more than one year. The stock market, government bonds markets and derivatives market are examples of capital market.

A third way of classification of financial markets is on the basis of seasoning of claim into primary market and secondary market.

Primary Markets

Primary markets are those markets, which deal in the new financial claims or new securities, and, therefore, they are also known as new issue markets. In simple words primary markets are the markets for the securities issued directly by the companies. Primary market, also known as New Issues Market (NIM), is a market for raising fresh capital in the form of shares and debentures. The primary markets mobilize savings and supply fresh or additional capital to business units.

Secondary markets

Secondary markets are those markets which deal in securities already issued or existing or outstanding. The secondary markets do not contribute directly to the supply of additional capital; they do so indirectly by rendering securities liquid which are issued on the primary markets.

A fourth way of classifying financial markets is on the basis of its structure or arrangements. They can be classified into organized markets and unorganized markets.

Organized Markets

The financial transactions which take place within the well established exchanges or in the systematic and orderly structure are called organised markets.

Unorganized Markets

The financial transactions which take place outside the well established exchanges or without systematic and orderly structure or arrangements are called unorganized markets.

A fifth way of classifying financial markets into cash/spot market, forward / future markets is by considering the timing of delivery.

Cash/Spot Market

Cash market is one where the buying and selling of commodities happens or stocks are sold for cash and delivered immediately after the purchase or sale of securities.

Forward or future market

Forward market is one where participants buy and sell stocks/ commodities, contracts and the delivery of securities occurs at a pre-determined time in future.

FINANCIAL INSTRUMENTS

Financial instruments are those instruments which are used for raising resources for corporate entities. The financial instruments may be capital market instruments or money market instruments. The financial instruments that are used for raising capital through the capital market are known as 'capital market instruments'. They are preference shares, equity shares, warrants, debentures and bonds. The financial instruments which are used for raising and supplying money in a short period not exceeding one year through various securities are called 'money market instruments', for example, treasure bills, gilt-edged securities, state government and public sector instruments, commercial paper, commercial bills etc.

FINANCIAL SERVICES

Financial services are an important component of a financial system. Financial services cater to the needs of financial institutions, financial markets and financial instruments. Financial institutions serve individuals and institutional investors. The financial institutions and financial markets help the financial system through financial instruments. They require a number of services of financial nature in order to fulfill the tasks assigned. The functioning of financial system very much depends on the range of financial services provided by the providers, and their efficiency.

Following are some of the functions of financial service institutions.

1. These firms not only help to raise the required funds but also assure the efficient deployment of funds.
2. They assist in deciding the financing mix.
3. They extend their service up to the stage of servicing of lenders.
4. They provide services like bill discounting, factoring of debtors, parking of short-term funds in the money market, e-commerce, securitization of debts, and so on to ensure an efficient management of funds.
5. These firms provide some specialized services like credit rating, venture capital financing, lease financing, factoring, mutual funds, merchant banking, stock lending, depository, credit cards, housing finance, and merchant banking and so on. These services are generally provided by banking companies, insurance companies, stock exchanges and non-banking finance companies.

FINANCIAL ASSETS

Financial assets represent a claim for the payment of a sum of money sometime in the future (repayment of principal) and /or a periodic (regular or not so regular) payment in the form of interest or dividend, e.g., bank deposit, government bond, industrial debenture, shares etc.

MONEY MARKET

Money market is a market for short-term funds; meant for short-term financial assets which are near-substitutes for money. The commercial banks comprising public sector banks (PSBs), private sector domestic and foreign banks, co-operative banks, regional rural banks (RRBs), play a vital role in money market. When market for funds is very short one day or overnight such market is called 'call money market'. In the call money market in addition to banks other institutions like investment institutions, companies also participate.

A money market is a mechanism through which short-term funds are loaned and borrowed and through which a large part of the financial transactions of a particular country or of the world are cleared.

Structure of Indian Money Market

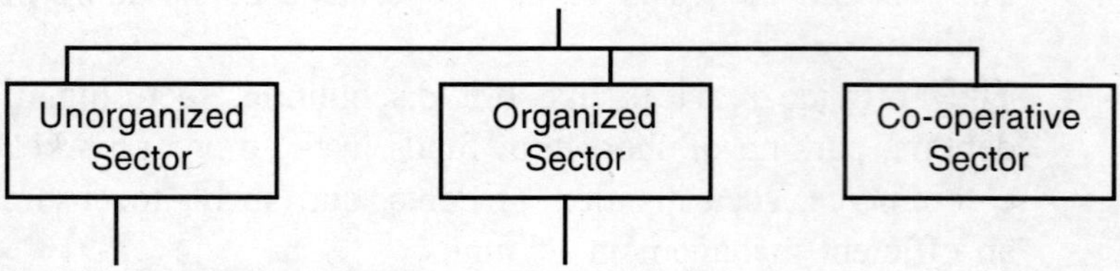

Unorganized Sector:

1. Indigenous Bankers
2. Moneylenders
3. Nidhi's
4. Chit funds

Organized Sector:

1. RBI
2. PSBs
3. Private sector banks, foreign & Indian banks
4. Developmental banks & other FIs like LIC, UTI, IFC, IDBI

General Characteristics of Money Market

The following are the characteristics of money market

1. Money market is basically over-the-phone market. It is confirmed later along with the documents.
2. Dealings in money market may be conducted with or without the help of brokers.
3. It is a market for short-term financial assets that are close substitutes for money.
4. Short term is generally a period up to one year.
5. Financial assets can be converted into money with ease, speed, without loss and with minimum transition cost.
6. Money market consists of many sub-markets, namely,
   a) Call Money Market
   b) Treasury Bills Market
   c) Commercial Bills Market
   d) Markets for Commercial Paper and Certificate of Deposits
   e) The Discount Market
   f) Markets for Futures, Options, and other Financial Derivatives

Objectives of Money Market

Following are the objectives of money market:

1. The money market provides an equilibrating mechanism for evening out short-term surpluses and deficits.
2. The money market provides a focal point for central bank intervention for influencing liquidity in the economy to control the interest rate fluctuation.
3. It provides reasonable access to users of short-term money to meet their requirements at a realistic price.

Prerequisites for an Efficient Money Market

For an efficient money market the following are the requirements:

Prerequisites of an Efficient Money Market

1. It should be wide and deep.
2. Well diversified mix of money market instruments.
3. Active secondary market for these instruments.
4. A strong central bank regulation.
5. Scope for market forces to determine interest rates.
6. Well organized commercial banking system.
7. Inter-related and integrated sub-markets.
8. Competition among sub-markets.
9. Adequate liquidity and ready marketability.
10. Large demand and supply for funds.

1. Money market should be wide and deep i.e., there should be adequate number of participants with an adequate supply of funds from within and from abroad.
2. There should be well-diversified mix of money market instruments, borrowers and lenders.
3. There should be active secondary market in these instruments. The success-money market always depends on the secondary market. If secondary market develops then there will be active trading of the instruments.
4. A strong central bank for regulation, direction and facilitation of money market.
5. A well organized commercial banking system. It increases the discipline in the market and also number of players in the market.
6. Money markets should offer opportunities to market forces in determining demand and supply of funds and the rates of interest.
7. There should be a number of inter-related and integrated sub-markets.
8. There should be competition within each sub-market as well as between different sub-markets.
9. Must have adequate amount of liquidity and ready marketability of instruments. It encourages players'

participation and also helps them to park their surplus funds and also to borrow the funds whenever there is requirement.

10. Money market should have a large demand and supply of funds. This depends upon the number of participants and also the policies of the government in encouraging the investments in various sectors and monetary policy of the RBI.

Importance of Money market

A well developed money market is required for the economic development of a country. Its importance is ascertained in the following ways.

Importance of Money Market
1. Source for financing trade and industry.
2. Influence on the resource mobilization and interest rate in capital market.
3. Helps commercial banks to park their surplus funds and borrowings.
4. Helps in effective implementation of monetary policy.
5. Non-inflationary avenue of raising short term funds.

1. It is an important source of financing trade and industry through bills, commercial papers. It influences the availability of finances both in the national and international trade.
2. Availability of funds in the money market and interest rates in the money market will influence on the resource mobilization and interest rate in capital market.
3. Money market helps commercial banks for investing their surplus funds and borrowing short-term funds to meet the statutory requirements of CRR & SLR.
4. It helps the central bank of a country to effectively implement its monetary policy.

5. It offers an important non-inflationary avenue of raising short-term funds to the government through bills which are subscribed by commercial banks and the public.

Capital Markets

Capital market may be defined as a market for borrowing and lending long-term capital funds required by business enterprises. Capital markets deal in the long-term claims (with a maturity period of more than one year). e.g., equity shares, preference shares, debentures, bonds, government securities, derivatives, swaps, future, options, etc. The capital market is once again classified into corporate securities market and government securities market or gilt-edged market.

INSTRUMENTS OF MONEY MARKET

Players in the money market, including commercial banks, mutual funds, investment institution, financial institutions and the RBI have various types of instrument through which they can borrow and lend money in the money market. These instruments are:

1. Call or Notice Money Market
2. Commercial Bill Market
3. Certificate of Deposits
4. Commercial Papers
5. Ready Forward Contracts
6. Treasury Bills Market
7. Discount Market
8. Money Market Mutual Funds (MMMFs)

1. Call Money Market

It is an important segment of the money market where the day-to-day surplus funds, mostly of banks, are traded in. The loans made in this market are of a short-term nature, their maturity varies between one day to a fortnight.

The characteristics of the call money market are:

1. Highly liquid. 2. Market for short-term funds. 3. Market is different in different countries. 4. Most sensitive segment of financial system. 5. Changes in demand and supply are quickly reflected in interest rates. 6. Effective operation of open market operations of RBI.

1. Call loans are repayable on demand and at the option of either the lender or the borrower or at very short notice. They are highly liquid.
2. Common characteristic of call money market is—it is a market for short-term funds.
3. This market is different in different countries based on
   (a) Institutional structure
   (b) Nature of participants
   (c) Purposes or types of transaction in such markets.
4. It is the most sensitive segment of financial system.
5. The changes in demand and supply of short-term funds get quickly reflected in call money interest rates.
6. The existence of an efficient call money market makes open market operations of RBI more effective.

If money is borrowed or lent for a day it is called ***call market*** or ***overnight market***. When money is borrowed or lent for more than a day and up to 14 days it is called ***short notice market.***

Participants in Call Money Market

The participants in the call money market are:

I. Those permitted to operate both as lenders and borrowers

(a) Commercial banks, both Indian and foreign
(b) Co-operative banks

(c) Discount and Finance House of India (DFHI)
(d) Securities Trading Corporation of India (STCI)
(e) Primary Dealers

II. Permitted Only to Operate as Lenders

Institutions that are LIC, UTI, GIC, IDBI, NABARD, specific institutions, which were operating in rediscounting market entities/ corporates/mutual funds with bulk lendable resources (10 crores) and private mutual funds.

2. Bill Market

Bill market is a specialized segment of the money market that deals in the purchase and sale of various types of commercial bill. Commercial bills are of two types: 1) bills of exchange and 2) treasury bills. Bills of exchange are important instruments, and are widely used in both domestic and foreign trade to discharge the business obligations. The bill of exchange is an unconditional order in writing signed by the seller, requiring the buyer to whom it is addressed, to pay on demand or at a fixed time in future, a definite sum of money to the order of seller or to the bearer. It is a negotiable instrument written by the creditor or seller, called drawer of the instrument for his debtor or buyer, who is called drawee. Once the debtor accepts the bill he becomes an acceptor and commits himself to make the payment of the amount specified in the bill, on the due date. These bills are also called 'trade bills'. Trade bills are called 'commercial bills' when they are accepted by commercial banks.

Since the bill is payable at a future date and the seller needs money, he may discount the bill with the bank. The banker will generally accept the bill at a discount to the face value. On the day of maturity the bill is presented for payment by the banker with the drawer of the bill, if the bill is discounted with the bank. These banks also re-discount the bills with other institutions like DFHI, commercial banks, mutual fund institutions, primary dealers etc.

3. Certificate of Deposits (CDs)

Certificate of Deposits represent short-term deposits which are transferable from one party to another. Banks and financial institutions are the major issuers of CDs. A CD takes the form of a receipt given by a bank or any other institution for funds deposited with it by the depositor. They generally have a maturity of 15 days to 1 year. CDs carry a certain interest rate.

Characteristics of CDs

1. CDs are negotiable short term-deposit certificates issued by commercial banks/financial institutions
2. These instruments are normally willing to tailor the denominations like 5 lakh each maximum of 25 lakh to each individual investor and also the maturities to suit the needs of the investor.
3. CDs are generally risk-free.
4. CDs generally offer a higher rate of interest than treasury bills or term deposits.
5. CDs require stamp duty, as is in the nature of usance note.

4. Commercial Papers (CPs)

A commercial paper represents short-term unsecured promissory note issued by firms that are generally considered to be financially strong. A commercial paper usually has a maturity period of 90 to 180 days. It is sold at a discount and is redeemed at par.

Characteristics of CPs

1. CPs are issued by the corporate in the form of promissory notes.
2. CP is issued at a discount to face value in multiples of 5 lakh.
3. It attracts stamp duty.
4. Issue of commercial paper requires mandatory rating as per the norms of RBI.

5. Interest rates prevailing in the call money market and foreign exchange market influence the marketability of CPs.
6. Satellite dealers are eligible to issue commercial papers with the prior approval of RBI. Satellite dealers are the dealers who are enlisted with the RBI to deal in the government securities market.

5. Ready Forward Contracts (REPOs)

The term Repo is used as an abbreviation for Repurchase Agreements or Ready Forward Contracts. A Repo involves a simultaneous "sale and repurchase" agreement. Repo rate is the rate at which the central bank lends short-term funds to the market (Repo). This rate was increased from 6.50 to 6.75 per cent on 8 June, by the RBI.

A Repo works as follows. Party A needs short-term funds and party B wants to make a short-term investment. Party A sells securities to Party B at a certain price and simultaneously agrees to repurchase the same after a specified time at a slightly higher price. The difference between the sale price and the repurchase price represents the interest cost to Party A (the party doing the Repo) and conversely the interest income for Party B (the party doing the reverse Repo).

6. Treasury Bill Market (TBs)

Treasury bills are an important instrument of short-term borrowing by the government. It is a tool of monetary management in the economy because their purchase and sale and yield rate on TBs has an impact on liquidity and the interest rate structure. TBs are the promissory notes or a kind of finance bill issued by the government under discount for a fixed period, not extending beyond one year.

Types of Treasury Bills in India

1. Ordinary or Regular TBs

The ordinary treasury bills are issued to the public, banks and other institutions for enabling the central government to raise resources for its short-term financial needs. These are freely marketable.

2. Ad hoc TBs

The ad hoc treasury bills are issued in favour of the RBI only. They are not sold through tender or auction. They are purchased by the RBI on tap and held in its Issue Department. The RBI is authorized to issue currency notes against these.

Purposes of issuing Treasury Bills are:

1. To replenish cash balances of Central Govt.
2. To provide investment outlet to state governments, semi-government departments and foreign banks.
3. Discount rate fluctuations, through selling them back to RBI. Auctions are avoided.

The following Treasury Bills are offered in India

1. 14 day T bill: The maturity of this bill is 14 days. Its auction is on every Friday of every week. The notified amount of this auction is Rs. 100 crores.
2. 91 day T bill: The maturity of this TB is 91 days. Its auction is on every Friday of every week. The notified amount of this auction is Rs. 100 crores
3. 182 days T bill: The maturity of this TB is 182 days. Its auction is on every alternative Wednesday (which is not a reporting week). The notified amount for this auction is Rs. 100 crores.
4. 364 days T bill: The maturity of this TB is 364 days. Its auction is on every alternative Wednesday (which is a reporting week). The notified amount for this auction is Rs. 500 crores.

Qualities of Treasury Bills

The following are the qualities of Treasury Bills

Qualities of Treasury Bills

1. High liquidity.
2. Zero default risk.
3. Ready availability on tap.
4. Low transaction cost.
5. Assured yield.
6. Eligible security for SLR.
7. Negligible scope for capital depreciation.

a) ***High liquidity***. The treasury bills are highly liquid. These can be converted into cash immediately by selling or by discounting.

b) ***Zero default risk***. The chance of default of treasury bills is zero, since it is issued by the central government.

c) ***Ready availability on tap from 1965***. The ad hoc treasury bills are issued at tap by the central government and purchased by the RBI whenever it is required to issue currency. It is issued through its Issue Department.

d) ***Low transaction cost***. The cost of issuing the treasury bills is very low since it doesn't involve stamp fee and also the issue of ad hoc treasury bill doesn't involve even auction or tender.

e) ***Assured yield***. The yield on the treasury bills is assured. It will not vary in any circumstances on which it is purchased.

f) ***Eligible security for SLR.*** It is an eligible security for statutory liquidity ratio which has to be maintained by all commercial banks.

g) ***Negligible scope of capital depreciation***. The chances of capital depreciation is nil in the case of investment on treasury bills.

Participants in TBs Market

The participants in the TBs market are RBI, SBI, commercial banks, state governments and other approved bodies, DFHI as a market maker, STCI, other financial institutions like LIC, UTI, GIC, NABARD, IBDI, IFCI etc., corporate entities, general public, foreign institutional investors since 1998.

Importance of TBs Market

I. To the Issuer / or Government

a. It is an important instrument for raising short-term funds for meeting temporary budget deficit.
b. The Government can mop up excess liquidity in the economy through issue of TBs.
c. Issue of TBs cannot lead to inflationary pressure since it is subscribed by investors other than the RBI.

II. To the Purchaser / Investor

a. It is a ready market for purchasers and investors.
b. The investors can invest their non-earning cash in TBs.
c. It is an eligible securitiy under SLR.
d. It is a safety instrument to invest.
e. Proper spread of asset mix with different maturities.
f. The yield on 365 days TBs is a benchmark for several floating rate bond issues issued by various PSUs.

7. Discount Market

The efficiency of the **money markets**, the efficiency of the **entire monetary system**, and the **ability of money market institutions** depend on the existence or availability of institutions, arrangements, and services for the best liquidity management. The participants in the money market must be in a position to command liquidity in times of need or crisis, and they must be in a position to even out the excesses or deficits in liquidity in different segments of the money market. Traditionally in all countries the central banks help banks in their liquidity management by providing them discounting and refinancing facilities. The Central Bank, however, is only the ultimate and in a sense an exogenous source of funds to the money markets.

In India, institutions like IDBI, NABARD, SIDBI, EXIM Bank, and NHB play an important role in the discount market before DFHI was established.

8. Money Market Mutual Funds (MMMFs)

Money Market Mutual Funds are those mutual funds which invest money primarily in money market instruments of very high quality and very short maturity. The RBI has approved the establishment of a few such funds in India. In 1997, only one MMMF was in operation, and that too with a very small amount of capital.

EXERCISE

Two marks questions

1. Mention the components of Indian financial system.
2. What is meant by financial system?
3. What do you mean by financial institutions?
4. Distinguish between financial institutions and non-financial institutions.
5. What do you mean by financial intermediary?
6. What do you mean by financial markets?
7. What do you mean by money market?
8. What is meant by capital market?
9. Distinguish between primary market and secondary market.
10. What do you mean by spot market and forward market?
11. What is meant by financial instruments?
12. What do you mean by financial services?
13. What do you mean by financial assets?
14. Mention any four instruments of money market.
15. What do you mean by commercial bills?
16. Distinguish between ordinary TBs and ad-hoc TBs.
17. What do you mean by call money market?
18. What do you mean by CPs?
19. What do you mean by CDs?
20. What do you mean by MMMFs?
21. What do you mean by Repos?

Five marks questions

1. Distinguish between banking institutions and non-banking institutions.
2. Classify and explain the financial markets.
3. What is meant by financial services? Explain its functions.
4. Briefly explain the qualities of treasury bills.

Fifteen Marks Questions

1. What is meant by financial system? Explain its structure.
2. What do you mean by money market? Explain its features and objectives.
3. Explain the prerequisites of efficient money market and bring out its importance.
4. Explain briefly the instruments of money market.
5. What do you mean by treasury bills? Why are they issued? Explain its importance.

Skill Development

1. Prepare a chart showing the structure of Indian financial system.
2. Prepare a list of non-banking financial institutions in India.
3. Make a list of ten financial instruments through which a company can raise its funds.
4. Make a chart showing structure of Indian banking system.
5. Prepare a list of ten financial services.
6. Classify 27 PSBs into nationalized banks and non-nationalised banks.
7. Prepare a list of existing New Generation Banks.
8. Take *Economic Times* and observe the terms used in the call money market, list and discuss with your friends.
9. Give a visit to the vegetable market of your location in a city and discuss with a vendor how he gets funds from the money vendor, how much interest he pays per day and compute the annual interest and compare this with the commercial banks rate of interest and discuss.
10. Prepare a list of money market instruments traded in India.

Chapter 2

COMMERCIAL BANKS

OUTLINE

- Role of Commercial Banks
- Structure of Indian Commercial Banks
- Functions
- Sources of Funds
- Investment Norms
- Motives of Investment Policy
- Assets Structure of Commercial Banks
- Profitability of Commercial Banks
  - Determinants of profitability
  - Profitability performance of commercial banks
  - Concepts used to measure the profitability

Question Bank
Skill Development

LEARNING OBJECTIVES

After reading the chapter you should be able to answer:

1. Role of commercial banks.
2. Structure of commercial banks in India.
3. Functions of commercial banks.
4. What are the sources of funds of commercial banks?
5. What are the investment norms in commercial banks?
6. Assets structure of commercial banks.
7. Motives of investment policy.
8. Factors determining liquidity.
9. Determinants of profitability.

ROLE OF COMMERCIAL BANKS

'Credit is the life and blood of commerce' and 'a bank is the mother of credit'. Commercial banks deal in money and credit, and thus occupy a very important place in the economic set-up of a country, specially under-developed ones. While many people believe that banks play only a narrow role in the economy—taking deposits and giving loans—on the contrary the modern banks have to adopt new roles in order to remain competitive and responsive to public needs. Following are the principal roles of modern banking: [1]

The intermediation role: Transforming savings received primarily from households into credit (loans) for business firms and others in order to make investments in new buildings, equipment, and other capital goods.

The payments role: Carrying out payments for goods and services on behalf of their customers (such as by issuing and clearing checks, wiring funds, and dispensing currency and coin.

The guarantor role: Standing behind their customers to pay off customer debts when those customers are unable to play (such as by issuing letters of credit).

The agency role: Acting on behalf of customers to manage and protect their property or issue and redeem their securities (usually provided through the banks trust department).

The policy role: Serving as a conduit for government policy in attempting to regulate the growth of the economy and pursue social goals.

From the economic point of view, the major task of banks and other financial institutions is to act as intermediaries channeling savings to investment and consumption: through them, the investment requirements of savers are reconciled with the credit needs of investors and consumers. When the Indian

---

[1] Peter S. Rose, "Commercial Bank Management", IRWIN series in finance, 3rd edition, 1996, p. 9.

situation is analysed the following two conclusions are clearly drawn.[2]

a) The Indian financial sector has considerably widened and deepened, thereby lending strong support to capital accumulation and overall economic growth.
b) The commercial banks in India constitute the single-most important component of the Indian financial system in bringing about the bulk of financial intermediation process in the country.

A significant part of this impressive record of financial development in India is attributable to the crucial role played by banks in the financial intermediation process. In India the financial sector comprises the banking system (i.e. commercial and co-operative banks), financial institutions (which include term lending institutions, i.e. IDBI, NABARD, ICICI, IRBI, IFCI, EXIM Bank and NHB at the all-India level and SFCs and SIDCs at the state level, besides investment institutions, i.e. UTI, LIC and GIC and other institutions including DICGC and ECGC), non-banking financial intermediaries and the capital market.

STRUCTURE OF INDIAN COMMERCIAL BANKS

Having established the pivotal role performed by the banking system in the Indian financial sector and by implication, in the overall financial intermediation process, thus supporting the real sector of the economy. The strong points of the financial system are its ability to mobilize savings, its vast geographical and functional reach and institutional diversity. Between 1965 and 1990, the household sector's gross savings in the form of financial assets rose from 5.5 per cent to 12.2 per cent of net domestic product. Since 1969 when major banks were nationalized, the number of commercial bank branches increased from about 8,300 to well over 65,000 by 2005.

---

[2] Narendra Jadhav (ed.), "Indian Banking: In Retrospect and Prospects" Challenges to Indian Banking—Competition, Globalisation and Financial Markets, Union Bank of India, 1996, p. 374.

Structure of Indian Banking System

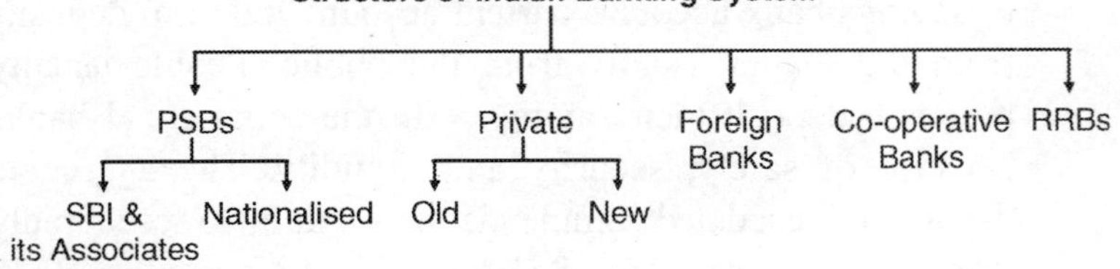

The commercial banking structure in India consists of: Scheduled Commercial Banks and Unscheduled Banks. Scheduled commercial banks constitute those banks, which have been included in the Second Schedule of Reserve Bank of India (RBI) Act, 1934. RBI includes only those banks in this schedule, which satisfy the criteria laid down vide section 42 (6) (a) of the Act. Indian banks can be broadly classified into nationalized banks/ public sector banks, private banks and foreign banks. The Indian banks include 27 public sector banks excluding 196 Regional Rural Banks (RRBs).

FUNCTIONS OF COMMERCIAL BANKS

Prof. Syers, defined banks as "institutions whose debt—usually referred to as 'bank deposits'—are commonly accepted in final settlement of other people's debts". According to Banking Regulation Act of 1949, "Banking means the accepting for the purpose of lending or investment of deposits of money from the public, repayable on demand or otherwise, and withdrawal by cheque, draft, order or otherwise". From the above definitions we can analyze that the primary functions of banks are accepting of deposits, lending of these deposits, allowing deposits to withdraw through cheque whenever they demand. The business of commercial banks is primarily to keep deposits and make loan and advances for short period up to one or two years made to industry and trade either by the system of overdrafts of an agreed amount or by discounting bills of exchange to make profit to the shareholders. From the above discussion, we can say that the following are the functions of commercial banks.

1. ***Receiving deposits from the public***. The primary function of commercial banks is receiving of deposits in the form of savings bank account, current account and term deposits from the savers usually from the public. People usually prefer to deposit their savings with the commercial banks because of safety, security and liquidity. The aggregate deposits of scheduled commercial banks in India rose rapidly from Rs. 822 crores in 1951 to Rs. 3,763 crores in 1967. The total deposits of commercial banks was Rs. 4,661 crores in 1969 that increased to Rs. 34,237 crores by 735 per cent by 1979. The total deposits of commercial banks increased in the decade of 1981 to 1991 from Rs. 40,413 crores to Rs. 2,00,569 crores by 5 times. Out of which the proportion of current, saving and fixed deposits were Rs. 6,286, Rs.11,805 and Rs. 22,322 crores which is almost 1: 2: 3 ratio increased to Rs. 30,335, Rs. 56,152 and Rs. 114082 crores i.e., almost 5 times during one decade with almost same proportion. The total deposits with commercial banks by the end of 2005 increased to Rs. 21,00,000 crores.
2. ***Giving loans and advances***. The second major function of the commercial banks is giving loans and advances to the all types of persons, particularly to businessmen and investors, against personal security, gold and sliver and other movable and immovable assets. The bank advances loans in the form of cash credit, call loans, overdraft and discounting bills of exchange to businessmen. After reforms in banking sector and establishment of new private sector banks and foreign banks, the other commercial banks also started giving loans and advances not only to their traditional businesses but also for vehicles, housing, consumer durables, etc. by increasing the base of lending activities.
3. ***Use of cheque system and credit cards***. The commercial banks will allow the depositors of the bank to withdraw and make payment of their amount in their bank account through cheques. Now the banks are allowed to use debit and credit cards for making their payments.

4. ***Credit creation***. Credit creation is one of the most important functions of the commercial banks. Like other financial institutions, they aim at earning profits. For this purpose they accept deposits and advance loans by keeping small cash in reserve for day-to-day transactions. When a bank advances a loan, it opens an account in the name of the customer and does not pay him in cash but allows him to draw the money by cheque according to his needs. By granting a loan, the bank creates credit or deposit.
5. ***Financing foreign trade***. The commercial banks finance foreign trade of its customers by accepting foreign bills of exchange and collecting them from foreign banks. It also transacts other foreign exchange business and buys and sells foreign currency.
6. ***Transfer of funds***. Commercial banks will help the customers to transfer their money from one account to another account, from one place to another place through cheques. Now the transfer of funds from one place to another place, or from one party account to another party account or one bank to another bank is done through Electronic Fund Transfer (EFT). This facility helps in transfering funds from one bank to another bank or to another party account easy. The technology like MICR helps the banks to have innovative banking like anywhere banking, anytime banking, and virtual banking and so on.
7. ***Agency functions***. The commercial banks act as agents for customers to buy and sell shares, securities on their behalf. It pays subscriptions to insurance premiums, mutual funds, rent, water taxes, electricity bills etc on behalf of its clients. It also acts as a trustee and executor of the property and will of its customers.
8. ***Miscellaneous functions***. The miscellaneous functions performed by the commercial banks are: it provides safety locker facility, making and receiving payments on behalf of its depositors, issuing letters of credit and traveller's cheques etc.

SOURCES OF FUNDS

The major source of funds of commercial banks is its deposits. Deposits are the life and blood of commercial banks as they are the mainstay of bank funds and account for about 90 per cent of bank liabilities. Credit creation and deployment depend upon deposits, which is very essential for the economic development. The banks act as intermediaries between the savers and users of funds. By pooling the savings together, banks can make available funds to specialized institutions that finance different sectors of the economy, which need capital for various purposes like agriculture, industries, housing etc.

Indian banks accept two main types of deposit—demand deposits and term deposits. Demand deposits can be sub-divided into two categories—Current and Savings. The growth of deposits of the banks depends upon various factors like:

a) Increase in National Income
b) Increase in relative rate of return on deposits
c) Expansion of banking facilities in new areas and for new classes of people
d) Increase in banking habit
e) Increase in deficit financing
f) Increase in bank credit
g) Inflow of deposits from NRIs
h) Growth of substitutes.

The other source of funds of commercial banks is borrowings from other banks. The commercial banks will borrow funds from other commercial banks when they have the problem for funds to maintain cash reserve ratio or to meet the temporary problem of liquidity due to more advances. Since the cost of these funds will be more, they go for this source as an alternative for temporary adjustment.

INVESTMENT NORMS

If we look at the balance sheet of a bank, investments constitute one of the important assets of the bank next to loans and advances. A bank makes investments for the purpose of earning profits. First it keeps primary and secondary reserves to meet its liquidity requirements. Banks invest in securities either for fulfilment of SLR/CRR requirements or for earning profit on the idle funds. Banks invest in "approved securities" (predominantly Government securities) and "others" (shares, debentures and bonds). The values/rates of these securities are subject to change depending on the market conditions. Some securities are transacted frequently and some are held till maturity. The Ghosh Committee recommended that "a bank's investment portfolio should be bifurcated into two parts, namely, 'permanent investment' and 'current investment'. The committee recommended that banks should make necessary provision for the depreciation in the value of current investment and there is no need to provide for permanent investment.

RBI has also advised the banks to classify the existing investment in approved securities into two categories. Initially from the accounting year 1992-93, banks should not keep more than 70% of their investment in permanent category, and 30% of the portfolio as current investments to facilitate valuing all the investments on fully 'marked to market' basis. Guidelines were laid down for transfer of approved securities from 'current' to 'permanent' and 'vice versa' in 1992. These guidelines ensure that latent losses are provided for at the time of such transfer. In 1993 the entire investment portfolio of banks other than investments classified as 'permanent' has to be classified into six categories for the purpose of valuation. The valuation will be done for each category of investments. While net depreciation has to be provided by debit to the profit and loss account, net gains have to be ignored. Permanent investments can be carried at book value. Premium will have to be amortized over the life of the investment but discount cannot be recognized as income. In between 1993 to 1998 the said minimum ratio of 30 per cent has been increased in a phased manner to 60 per cent as on March 31, 1998. It has further been decided to increase the ratio to 70 per cent for the year ending March 31, 1999. New private sector banks are required to market their entire investments in approved securities since March 31, 1997.

MOTIVES OF INVESTMENT POLICY

The commercial banks have to follow the guidelines issued by RBI for investments. The following are the motives of investment policy of RBI.

1. ***Safety and security***. Safety and security of the funds which are deposited by the customers of the bank is very important in banks. The money which is deposited by the customers in banks should be safe and they should get back whenever they require. The banks should see that the money which is deposited in commercial banks should not be misused by the banks through its unscrupulous management or mismanagement and lead to loss and consequently lead to bankruptcy. Hence the RBI will guide the commercial banks through its monetary policies and issues guidelines to follow in their investment policies. To safeguard the interests of the depositors in commercial banks the deposits are insured up to Rs. 1,00,000.
2. ***Liquidity of funds in banks.*** Commercial banks have to maintain liquidity of funds deposited by the depositors of the banks. The banks should see that the money deposited is allowed by the banks to withdraw whenever the customers require during working hours of the bank. This will ensure more confidence among the customers of the bank. There are several cases where Indian commercial banks ensured liquidity to the depositors of the bank. Recently during 2001 the rumours spread among the customers of the ICICI Bank in Maharashtra that there is no cash in the bank. Hence many customers went for withdrawing of the funds deposited and the ATM counters were flooded with customers. The bank also made arrangements for cash and also assured the customers not to panic. Immediately the RBI assured that there is no liquidity problem in the bank. Hence liquidity in banks is a

very important motive of the investment policy. Therefore banks are directed to keep some percentage of the funds in the form of Cash Reserve Ratio in RBI and also insist to invest in Statutory Liquid Ratio to convert into easy liquidity.

3. ***Profitability of the bank.*** The soundness of any bank is measured by its profitability. The customers will come forward to deposit their funds with banks on the basis of the profitability of the banks. Hence the banks have to earn profits.

Factors Determining Liquidity of Banks

The liquidity of a bank is determined by the top management of the bank on the basis of the nature of business conditions in a country. This is also guided by the central bank of that country to ensure liquidity in an economy. The extent of liquidity is ensured on the basis of the following factors.

1. ***The size of liquid reserves***. The size of the liquid reserves will depend upon the extent of liquid reserves considered essential by the banking community. If the liquid reserves in a bank will increase the liquidity position of the banks but the amount available for lending will decrease. During the year 1991 to 1995 the CRR of the commercial banks with the RBI was 15 to 14.5 percent on Net Demand and Time Liabilities (NDTL), hence the amount available with the banks for lending was less hence it hampered the growth of our economy. By realizing this problem RBI after accepting reform process in the economy reduced this ratio. Since then the amount available for lending with the banks has increased, consecutively the Credit Deposit (CD) ratio also increased. It was around 56 percent during 2004 it went up to 71 per cent during the month of February 2006 by showing good symptom of growth in the credit activities in an economy.
2. ***Banking habits of the people.*** Liquidity of a bank depends upon the banking habits of people. If the country is

developed then the people will have the habit of doing the business through cheques or credit cards. In these countries the liquidity of banks need not be more. Whereas in the case of people in underdeveloped countries they use cash more than the cheques or credit cards in their transactions hence the requirement of liquidity will be more.

3. ***Number and magnitude of monetary transactions in the country.*** The liquidity in banks depends on the number and magnitude of monetary transactions in the country. If the number and magnitude of monetary transactions are more then the requirement of liquidity in banks should be more otherwise it is vice-versa.
4. ***Nature of business conditions.*** If the business conditions in an economy are good then the liquidity position in an economy will be more. During prosperity or boom period the business transactions will be more and hence the flow of funds with the individuals and in the country will be high, this is also because of good earning capacity of the people. This we have experienced when we opened our economy for LPG. During the period 1992 to 1997 and later funds in our economy started flowing hence the business in Indian, both rural and urban sectors, improved, that led to the improving the liquidity position in the banking and in other sectors.
5. ***Structure of banking system.*** The structure of banking system is the other factor which will have its influence on the liquidity in the banks. If the structure of the banks is branch banking the number of banks will be more and also these branches are spread throughout the country both in urban and rural areas which will increase the liquidity in banks. If the structure of the banking system is unit banking naturally the liquidity position of these banks will be comparatively less. In addition in India we have RRBs, co-operative banks—these will help in improving the liquidity position of the banks.

6. ***Well organized money market.*** Well organized and developed money market is another factor which will have its influence on the liquidity position of the banks. If the money market is well organized, the commercial banks will borrow and lend their cash in the money market which reduces the idle money with the banking sector and also supports the liquidity position in the banking sector and also in an economy.

ASSET STRUCTURE OF COMMERCIAL BANKS

Assets structure will reflect the deployment of sources of funds of commercial banks. The main source of funds of commercial banks is deposits. The other sources of funds are borrowings from other banks, capital, reserves and surplus. The deposits of commercial banks are from savings deposits, current account deposits and term deposits. These deposits constitute 80 per cent of the total sources of funds. Out of the total deposits, term deposits constitute 50 per cent. Borrowings are around 5 per cent of the total liabilities of the commercial banks. These sources are deployed by the commercial banks mainly on its financial assets i.e, loans and advances which constitute 48.6 per cent of the total assets of the banks. The investments is another important component of the assets of commercial banks which is around 40 per cent of the total assets of the banks during the year 2005. This is because of pre-emptions like SLR and CRR requirements in the banking sector. The investments in commercial banks have increased also because of surplus liquidity in Indian banks during this period due to reduction of SLR and CRR to 25 and 4.5 respectively during that period and less demand for loans and advances from credit-worthy customers. This scenario is changing in India due to increasing demand in credit from industrial, agriculture sector and also the growth of FMCG market.

The assets structure of the banks is governed by certain principles, like liquidity, profitability, shiftability and risklessness. The other factors which influence the assets structure of

Consolidated Balance Sheet of Scheduled Commercial Banks

Sl. no	Liabilities / Assets	2004 Amount in Rs. Crore	Per cent to total	2005 Amount in Rs. Crore	Per cent to total
1.	Capital	22,348	1.1	25,183	1.1
2.	Reserves and Surplus	94,254	4.8	1,18,326	5.2
3.	Deposits	15,78,450	80.0	18,21,884	80.1
	Demand Deposits	2,03,237	10.3	2,30,709	10.1
	Savings Bank Deposits	3,73,677	18.9	4,43,052	19.5
	Term Deposits	10,01,536	50.7	11,48,123	50.5
4.	Borrowings	95,562	4.8	1,18,311	5.2
5.	Other Liabilities and Provisions	1,83,402	9.3	1,90,918	8.4
	Total Liabilities	**19,74,017**	**100.0**	**22,74,622**	**100.0**
	Assets				
	Cash and Balances with RBI				
1.	Balances with Banks and	1,13,246	5.7	1,15,711	5.1
2.	Money at Call and Short Notice	82,033	4.2	92,927	4.1
3.	Investments	8,04,199	40.7	8,43,081	37.1
	In Government Securities	6,39,143	32.4	6,84,005	30.1
	In Other Approved Securities	18,100	0.9	16,291	0.7
	In Non-approved Securities	1,46,956	7.4	1,42,785	6.3
4.	Loans and Advances	8,64,271	43.8	11,05,725	48.6
5.	Fixed Assets	21,409	1.1	22,161	1.0
6.	Other Assets	88,860	4.5	95,018	4.2
	Total Assets	**19,74,017**	**100.0**	**22,74,622**	**100.0**

commercial banks are nature of money market, economic growth of the country, policies and vision of the governments. In the countries like India, China, Russia, North Korea and Brazil there is a boom in the growth of the economy hence naturally there will be heavy demand for the credit.

Now let us examine each of the important assets of the commercial bank.

1. **Cash in hand and balances with RBI**. From the point of the liquidity in the commercial banks cash in hand is a very important asset but it is idle and it will not fetch any earnings to the banks. Cash in commercial banks depends upon various factors like uncertainty in the economy due to wars, famine, internal disturbance, the growth of banking system, network of branches, networking of banks, automation in banks and so on. The cash reserve requirements in the commercial banks was more during pre-reform period it was 15 per cent during the year 1994-95. Gradually RBI reduced it to 4 per cent based on the requirements of credit and it is now 5 per cent on Net Demand and Time Liabilities.
2. **Money at Call and Short Notice.** It is second line of defense of the commercial banks in cases of emergencies. If the call money market is well developed the commercial banks can lend their surplus funds in the call market for a day or up to 14 days it is called call market or over night market without keeping their surplus money idle. It can also lend for short period, where the borrower has to return the money borrowed from the banks when short notice is given by the banks. This is becoming a good business in the money market and constitutes around 4 per cent of the total assets of the commercial banks. The banks instead of keeping the money idle lend their surplus funds for short periods in the call market.
3. **Investments.** Investments constitute one of the important assets of the bank next to loans and advances. A bank makes investments for the purpose of earning profits. First,

it keeps primary and secondary reserves to meet its liquidity requirements. Banks invest in securities either for fulfilment of SLR/CRR requirements or for earning profit on the idle funds. Banks invest in "approved securities" (predominantly Government securities) and "others" (shares, debentures and bonds). The values/rates of these securities are subject to change depending on the market conditions. Some securities are transacted frequently and some are held till maturity. Total investments during the year 2005 by the commercial banks in India were Rs. 8,43,081 crores which is 37 per cent of the total assets. During the month of February and March 2006 the investments in Indian commercial banks have reduced because of heavy demand for credit. Some banks even sold their surplus investments in government securities which was more than SLR requirements and converted them into cash for lending.

4. **Loans and Advances.** The commercial banking industry in India has been playing a very important role in intermediating between the economic units, which have surpluses and deficits in their current budgets. By mobilizing financial surpluses in the economy and by channeling these resources into various sectors and segments of the economy, they are guiding the pattern of utilisation of a large proportion of the economy. The Government of India which owns a large segment of the industry, and the RBI, which is the central banking authority of the country, have been persuading the commercial banks to deploy larger and larger volumes of financial resources into certain identified priority sectors, for the purpose of accelerating the growth of these sectors. The total advances of commercial banks include bills purchased and discounted, cash credits, overdrafts, loans, unsecured loans, and priority sector advances. The component of loans and advances in the total assets of commercial banks is 48 to 50 per cent—in fact still growing in India. The management of this asset is a very important aspect in the banking sector. The non-performing assets in

banks is increasing. In addition to this banks are exposed to various risks such as credit risk, liquidity risk, market risk and operational risk.

5. **Fixed Assets and other assets.** The component of fixed assets and other assets do not form an important aspect in the funds of commercial banks since deals are more in financial assets than real assets.

PROFITABILITY OF COMMERCIAL BANKS

Profitability is a key parameter in assessing the performance of any business firm. Even in the banking sector after the banking sector reforms the priorities in banking operations underwent far reaching changes. There had been a shift in the emphasis from development or social banking to commercially viable banking. Profitability became the prime mover of the financial strength and performance of banks; hence the performance of the bank is measured on the basis of its profitability. Now the main agenda is to enhance the profitability and reduce the hurdles which are faced by the banks in their profit maximization and to develop strategies to achieve this objective. In this changed scenario, profitability and productivity are the twin indicators of the competitive edge of the banking industry.

The main reason for the fundamental paradigm shift in the banking from social banking to "profit banking" was the introduction of capital adequacy requirements. There are four ways to achieve and sustain the required capital adequacy: fresh equity issue, ploughing back of profit, debt offering and revaluation of assets. Raising capital through equity route is very difficult because servicing the equity base, offering reasonable returns, raising fresh capital when the capital market is not favourable and when the performance of banks is not good. Similarly debt raising also will have the limitations too, as tier II capital cannot exceed tier I capital and subordinated debt cannot exceed 50% of the tier II capital. The scope of revaluation of assets for improving capital adequacy is limited and hence banks are left with the outré of ploughing back of profits as an efficient tool to reach and sustain the capital adequacy ratio.

Determinants of Profitability

The various macro level as well as unit specific factors which have an impact on the profitability of the banks are given below.[2]

Macro level factors

1. **Allocational Efficiency**. Allocational efficiency has an impact on bank profitability. Allocational efficiency refers to the efficient deployment of funds among competing demands so as to maximize returns while minimizing risks involved. SLR, CRR, directed credit at concession rates, nursing of sick borrower accounts, limits to individual units and groups of companies which affect the allocational efficiency of banks.
2. **Level of disintermediation**. Disintermediation is just opposite to intermediation. In disintermediation the commercial banks will lose the customer base because of opting out of other sources by the borrowers like Foreign Direct Investments (FDI), Commercial Papers, public deposits by the companies and so on. Commercial banks will lose both revenue and cost front as a result of the growth in disintermediation. The growth of disintermediation will reduce the revenue of the banks because of the reduction in interest spreads.
3. **Volume of credit and profitability**. Volume of credit in the banking system is determined by growth in savings, level of SLR and CRR, level of disintermediation, capital markets, economic and industrial growth. The income from

---

[2] Ramamoorthy. K.R. "Profitability and Productivity in Indian Banking–International Comparisons and Implications for Indian Banking", Proceedings of the Bank Economisats' Conference 1997.

fee-based activities like letters of credit, guarantees, and acceptance commission is also responsible for growth in profitability of the banks now-a-days because of thin interest margin.

4. **Provisioning for loan losses, loan quality improvements or non-Performing Assets**. Provisioning for loan losses and non-performing assets reduce the profitability of the banking system. NPAs, reduces the net profits of banks on account of loss in income and the provisioning for NPAs will reduce the profit of the banks.
5. **Interest rate movements**. Interest rate movements affect the net interest margins of the banks. A net interest margin refers to difference between interest on deposits and interest on advances. When interest rates increase, the impact is immediate on the advances, which reduces the demand for advances and reduces the profits of the banks. The change in interest rates are exposed to interest rate risks and asset-liability mismatches, which calls for Asset Liability Management (ALM).
6. **Rigidity of the operating cost structure**. About 60 to 70 per cent of the operating costs of Indian commercial banks is on account of employee costs. The other significant cost components are real estate and technology costs. These costs are non-controllable to a significant extent and are rising constantly hence, reducing the profitability of banks.

Unit Specific factors

1. **Banking structure**. Structure of the banking system will have its impact on the profitability of banks. The diversified banking structure with operations spread across regions having different economic/business profiles, like Indian public sector banks will have higher operating costs in view of a larger network, lower margins due to greater competition.
2. **Size of Bank**. Indian situation suggests that when banks are considered groups in terms of big, medium and small, the bigger banks have greater scope for economies of scale.

The per centages of total expenses to working funds are lower for bigger size banks than for small size banks. Whereas in other countries like European Investment Banks, a study of American and Japanese banks have observed that there is no convincing correlation between the size of banks and earning power.

3. **Branch network or Franchise strength**. A large network of branches located at potential centres provides access to low cost deposits as well as increased scope for earning more fee-based income in the form of commission on remittance services and bills for collection.

Profitability Performance of Commercial Banks

Profitability is one major criterion for evaluating the performance of banks. If profitability has to be planned and improved, detailed, systematic and objective analysis is necessary. It calls for studying the factors determining profitability, how they behave, how they are related to each other and how valid inter-bank comparisons are.

To evaluate the profitability performance of the banks largely ratios are used as a tool for comparison. There is no unanimity in the selection of ratios. The ratios usually used are:

1. Net Profit / Net Worth
2. Spread / Working Funds
3. Burden / Working Funds
4. Interest Income / Total Earning Assets
5. Non-Interest Income / Total Earning Assets
6. Interest Expenses / Total Earning Assets
7. Non-Interest Expenditure (Operating Expenditure) / Total Earning Assets
8. Net Profit / Working funds
9. Net Non-Performing Assets / Net advances
10. Capital Adequacy Ratio
11. Savings Deposit / Total Deposits
12. Current Deposits / Total Deposits
13. Term Deposits / Total Deposits

14. Priority Sector Advances / Total Advances
15. Deposits per Employee
16. Advances per Employee

Concepts used to Measure the Profitability

1. **Spread is defined as the difference between interest earned and interest paid.** Spread and non-interest income earned as commission and service charged constitute the revenue pool out of which manpower and other expenses are met. The balance constitutes the profit (or loss). The spread is analogous to gross profit in the Trading Account of a trading concern. It plays, therefore, a major role in determining the profitability of a bank. Variation in spread indicates whether a bank has positioned its assets and liabilities to take advantage of rate changes (interest rate), that is, whether it has actually profited or lost when interest rates got increased or declined.
2. **Burden** is the excess of non-interest expenses over non-interest income. The profit (or loss) of a bank is determined by the spread and burden.
3. **Interest income** constitutes interest and discount received on their earning assets. The Total Earning assets[3] are calculated by dividing the Non-Earning Assets by the Total Assets. The non-earning assets are cash and balance with RBI, cash in hand, fixed assets, other assets and contra items
4. **Non-interest income** constitutes Commission Exchange and Brokerage, Revaluation and sale of investments, exchange transactions, income earned by dividends miscellaneous income etc. As competition for loans and other income-generating assets has grown and many loans have turned sour (NPAs), more and more banks have

---

[3] Peter S. Rose, "Commercial Bank Management", IRWIN Series in Finance, 3rd Edition, 1996. p. 168.

shifted their attention to increasing non-interest income from fees. This fee based total revenue helps to raise net income flowing to bank stockholders.

5. **Interest expense** constitutes interest paid on deposits, RBI/inter-bank borrowings and others.
6. **Non-interest expenses** are also called operating expenses or overhead, which constitutes expenses incurred for establishment, rent, taxes and lighting, printing and stationery, advertisement, depreciation etc.

In order to evaluate the performance of the commercial banks the Reserve Bank of India uses CAMEL method. The prime task of regulatory agencies is to frame regulations and examine their adherence by banks through the examination process. This will help the RBI to evaluate how far a particular commercial bank has compliance with the guidelines. This is a major strategy in enhancing the control mechanism, supervision by the regulatory authorities. Central banks address to the issue by on-sight and off-sight inspections/examinations.

CAMEL refers to:

C = Capital Adequacy Ratio
A = Assets Ratios
M = Management Ratios
E = Earning Ratios.
L = Liquidity Ratios

EXERCISE

Two marks questions

1. Show the structure of commercial banks in India.
2. What do we mean by commercial banks?
3. What do we mean by intermediation role of banks?
4. What is payments role of banks?
5. Mention the agency role of banks.
6. Mention the sources of funds of commercial banks.
7. Mention the types of deposits of banks.

8. What is the policy role of banks?
9. What is liquidity in banks?
10. What do you mean by Spread?
11. What is meant by Burden?
12. What are the components of other incomes of banks?
13. What do we mean by interest margin?
14. What CAMEL stands for in Banks?

Five marks questions

1. Mention the functions of commercial banks.
2. Discuss the motives of investment policy of commercial bank.
3. What are the sources of funds of commercial banks?
4. Examine the structure of assets of banks.
5. Mention the factors determining liquidity.
6. Mention some important ratios used to evaluate the performance of the banks.
7. Why CAMEL system is used in banks?
8. What are the determinants of profitability? Explain.

Fifteen marks questions

1. Explain the role of commercial banks.
2. What are the functions of commercial banks? Explain.
3. What are the sources of funds and how they are utilized?
4. What are the investment norms in commercial banks?
5. Explain the assets structure of commercial banks.
6. What are the motives of investment policy? Explain.
7. Why liquidity in commercial banks is significant? Explain the factors determining liquidity.
8. What are the macro and unit level determinants of profitability? Explain.

Skill Development

1. If a bank receives Rs. 1000 deposit, illustrate as a fund manager how do you manage this Rs. 1000 by maintaining CRR, SLR?
2. Collect annual report of a bank and compute the percentage of capital, of deposits, & of borrowing to total liabilities & also calculate percentage of each type of deposit to total deposits.
3. From the balance sheet of a bank compute various ratios and analyze.

Chapter 3
FINANCIAL INSTITUTIONS

OUTLINE

- Meaning and Role of Financial Institutions
- Industrial Development Bank of India
  - Objectives
  - Functions
- State Financial Corporations
  - Functions of SFCs
  - Schemes and working
  - Financial resources
  - SFCs (Amendment) Act, 2000
- State Industrial Development Corporations (SIDCs)
  - Functions
- Mutual Funds in India
  - Meaning
  - Computation of NAV
  - Classification of types of schemes
  - Functions
  - Benefits
- Unit Trust of India
  - Mobilization of saving
  - Diversification of activities
- Life Insurance Corporation of India
- EXIM Bank of India
  - Functions and objectives of establishment

LEARNING OBJECTIVES

After reading this chapter you should able to answer:

- What is the role of financial institutions?
- Growth, objectives and functions of IDBI.

- Working of SFCs in India and the changed trends in its functioning.
- Functions of SIDCs.
- Working of mutual fund industry in India.
- Functions and benefits of Mutual Funds.
- UTI and its working.
- Functions and objectives of EXIM Bank.

MEANING AND ROLE OF FINANCIAL INSTITUTIONS

Financial institutions are also known as financial intermediaries which provide the means and mechanism of transferring the resources from those whose income is more than expenditure to those who need these resources for investing in productive activities for productive capital. The savings of the savers will reach the borrower through the financial intermediaries as productive capital in the form of creating claims against themselves in the form of instruments like shares, debentures, stocks, deposits, certificates, bonds, secured loans and so on. Similarly they acquire claims against the investors by investing in their shares and debentures and by granting direct loans to them. In this way the financial institutions originated and started playing the role of intermediator between the savings and investments. This financial institution provides safety, liquidity and ensures return for savings.

The role of these financial institutions in the post-independence era was very important in mobilizing the savings. These institutions developed the saving habit of the people and mobilized huge amount of savings for the industrial development as a productive capital. There was a big gap between the supply of savings in the economy and demand for investments. To fill this gigantic gap of industrial needs, the financial institutions have played a very important role in India. Hence many financial institutions were floated by the Government of India, state governments and Reserve Bank of India. The following are the financial institutions in India.

1. Industrial Development Bank of India (IDBI)
2. Industrial Finance Corporation of India (IFCI)
3. Export-Import Bank of India (EXIM Bank)
4. Industrial Investment Bank of India
5. National Bank for Agriculture and Rural Development (NABARD)
6. Small Industries Development Bank of India (SIDBI)
7. National Housing Bank (NHB)
8. Unit Trust of India (UTI)
9. Life Insurance Corporation of India (LIC)
10. General Insurance Corporation of India (GIC)
11. Risk Capital and Technology Finance Corporation Ltd. (RCTC)
12. Technology Development and Information Company of India Ltd.(TDICI)
13. Tourism Finance Corporation of India Ltd. (TFCI)
14. Shipping Credit and Investment Company of India Ltd. (SCICI)
15. Discount and Finance House of India Ltd. (DFHI)
16. Securities Trading Corporation of India Ltd. (STCI)
17. Power Finance Corporation Ltd.
18. Rural Electrification Corporation Ltd.
19. Indian Railways Finance Corporation Ltd.
20. Infrastructure Development Finance Co. Ltd.
21. Housing and Urban Development Corporation Ltd. (HUDCO)
22. Indian Renewable Energy Development Agency Ltd. (IREDA)

These institutions have supplied capital to the small, medium and large scale industries in India in the form of capital, venture capital, services to foster the industrial growth in India. These have contributed magnificently for the growth and development of industries. Some of them are discussed here.

INDUSTRIAL DEVELOPMENT BANK OF INDIA (IDBI)

The Industrial Finance Corporation of India (IFCI), State Financial Corporations (SFCs) and Industrial Credit and Investment Corporation of India (ICICI) have been functioning for several years with the objective of providing direct loans, subscribing to shares and debentures of industrial businesses, underwriting of shares and bonds and guaranteeing of loans and deferred payments. In spite of growth of the term loans by these institutions, it was found that these institutions could not meet the full requirements of new and growing industrial enterprises. On the other hand the needs of industrialization in India necessitated the establishment of large financial institutions to cater to the needs of large resources required by these industries. In addition to the above needs there was a need for coordinating the activities of all agencies which were concerned with the provision of financing for industrial development. Therefore IDBI was established. The Industrial Development Bank is a specialized institution established in India in 1964 by the RBI as a wholly owned subsidiary to provide long-term finance to industrial enterprises. The RBI transferred its ownership to Government of India in 1976. The Government shareholding in IDBI came down to 51.4 percent after the public issue.

During the four decades of its existence, IDBI has been instrumental in establishing a well developed, diversified and efficient industrial and institutional structure. It also adds a qualitative dimension to the process of industrial development in the country. The cumulative assistance sanctioned and disbursed by IDBI since inception up to the end of September 2004 aggregated around Rs. 2,23,000 crores and Rs. 1,78,000 crores respectively. The asset base of IDBI at the end of September 2004 was Rs. 63,850 crores.

Objectives

The IDBI was launched with the following objectives.

1. To coordinate, supplement and integrate the activities of

existing financial institutions, specially to refinance term loans and export credits.

2. To conduct techno-economic studies and offer loans on purpose and not merely on security.

Functions of IDBI

The main function of IDBI is to give financial assistance to public and private sector industrial enterprises. A few of which get financial assistance are manufacturing, mining, processing, shipping, transport, and hotel industries. The financial assistance is provided either directly or through specified financial institutions.

1. **Direct Assistance.** It assists industrial units directly by way of project loan, underwriting of and direct subscription to industrial securities (shares and debentures), soft loans, technical development fund loans and equipment finance loans.
2. **Coordinating Function.** The IDBI will coordinate the functions and operations of all the financial institutions, including the IFCI, ICICI, LIC, GIC, UTI and so on into a single integrated financial structure so that each may contribute to the total growth of an economy.
3. **Indirect Assistance.** Indirect assistance is provided by IDBI to tiny, small and medium enterprises mainly by way of
   a) Granting term loans and advances.
   b) Refinance of finance of industrial loans granted by SFCs, SIDCs, commercial banks, co-operative banks and RRBs.
   c) Rediscounting of bills relating to the sale of indigenous machinery on deferred payment basis, and
   d) Seed capital assistance to new entrepreneurs through SFCs and SIDs.
   e) It raises foreign funds from international money markets and funding organization makes them available to those industrial units that need them.

4. **Special Assistance.** IDBI will assist the industrial concerns which are not able to get funds in the normal course because of heavy investment, low rate of return etc. out of its Development Assistance Fund.
5. **General Functions.** The banks can undertake promotional activities such as marketing, marketing research, feasibility study, techno-economic studies, managerial assistance and feasiblity study for expansion of activities.

Diversification of Activities of IDBI

Since 1990s IDBI has established a number of institutions, some of them are.

a) Small Industries Development Bank of India (SIDBI) in 1990
b) IDBI Investment Management Company Ltd. (IIMCO) in 1994
c) IDBI Capital Market Services Ltd. (ICMS) in 1995
d) IDBI Bank Limited in 1994

Assistance Sanctioned and Disbursed by IDBI (Rs. Crore)

Period	Amount	Amount
1993-94	12086.0	8095.9
1994-95	1819.9	10671.8
1995-96	16476.4	10695.2
1996-97	15634.0	11467.7
1997-98	23982.0	15170.0
1998-99	23744.7	14470.1
1999-2000	26966.5	17059.4
2000-01	26832.6	17476.9
2001-02	15867.9	11012.5
2002-03	5898.2	6614.9
2003-04	3937.7	4986.4
2004-05	16488.8	6882.2

Source:

STATE FINANCIAL CORPORATIONS (SFCs)

The state level financial institutions play an important role in the development of small and medium enterprises. The first state financial corporation was set up by the Madras government, which started Madras Industrial Investment Corporation therein it is called Tamilnadu Industrial Investment Corporation in 1949. Now we have 18 SFCs out of which 17 SFCs were established under the SFCs Act 1951.These SFCs function like the development banks in relation to small and medium enterprises.

Functions of SFCs

The functions of SFCs are:

1. They provide ***financial assistance*** to small-scale industries by way of term loans for a period not exceeding 20 years.
2. The SFCs directly ***subscribe to equity shares/debentures*** repayable within 20 years.
3. The SFCs ***guarantee loans*** raised by industrial concerns.
4. The SFCs also ***undertake the underwriting*** of the issues of stocks, shares, bonds, debentures etc.
5. They ***discount*** the bills of small and medium scale industries by performing a function of discounting of bills.
6. The SFCs provide ***seed/special capital*** at the beginning of the Small and Medium Entrepreneurs (SMEs).
7. They provide ***special schemes*** for artisans and special target groups like SC/ST, women, ex-servicemen, physically handicapped etc.
8. They provide ***loans for setting up new industrial units*** as well as for expansion and modernization of the existing units.
9. The schemes covered under SFCs are for floriculture, tissue culture, poultry farming, commercial complexes, and services relating to engineering, marketing etc.
10. ***The SFCs have gone for diversification of activities*** to equipment leasing, merchant-banking, debenture-trusteeship and capital market related services for providing better and different services and to earn profits.

Eligibility to avail services under SFCs

The eligibility criteria to avail credit facilities under State Financial Corporations are. They should be:

1. Public limited companies.
2. Private limited companies.
3. Co-operative societies.
4. Partnership firms.
5. Sole-proprietary or HUF which are engaged in industrial activities like manufacturing, preserving of goods, mining, hotel industry, generation, maintenance, providing technical knowledge or service, weigh bridge facilities, R & D etc.

Schemes offered by the SFCs

The SFCs offer schemes for:

1. Small scale units
2. Medium scale
3. Modernization of industrial units relating to:
   a) Upgradation of process, technology and product
   b) Export orientation
   c) Import substitution
   d) Energy saving
   e) Anti-pollution
   f) Conservation
4. IDBI Bill Rediscounting scheme
5. Composite loan scheme.

Working of SFCs

The State Financial Corporations which are established for serving the small and medium industries played a very important role in developing cottage, small and medium scale industries in India. The SFCs have sanctioned Rs. 2908 crores during 1993-94 and disbursed Rs. 1563 crores. During the year 1995-96 the sanctions were increased to Rs. 4188 crores with a growth rate of 50 percent and sanctions also increased to Rs. 2961 crores with a growth rate of 57.4 percent. Over the years the amount of sanctions and disbursements has decreased over the years as shown in the table.

Assistance Sanctioned and Disbursed by SFCs (Rs. Crore)

Period	Sanctioned Amount	Disbursement Growth rate %	Amount	Growth rate %
1993-94	1908	-5.3	1563	0.4
1994-95	2702	41.6	1881	20.3
1995-96	4188	55.0	2961	57.4
1996-97	3544	-15.4	2783	-6.0
1997-98	2628	-25.8	2118	-23.9
1998-99	1864	-29.0	1627	-22.9
1999-2000	2395	28.5	1843	13.3
2000-01	2911	21.6	1979	7.4
2001-02	2210	-24.1	1750	-11.6
2002-03	1855.9	-69.8	1454.0	-30.6
2003-04	1133.8	-115.55	856.8	-49.6

Source: Handbook of Statistics on the Indian Economy, RBI 2004-05.

Financial Resources of SFCs.

The financial resources of SFCs comprise the following:

1. **Capital Structure**: The capital structure of a SFC being determined by the state governments concerned, the minimum and maximum capitals will be Rs. 50 lakhs and Rs. 5 crores respectively.
2. **Contribution of Capital funds**: The capital funds are contributed by respective State Governments, the Industrial Development Bank of India (IDBI), scheduled commercial banks, state cooperative banks, insurance companies, investments trusts and the public.
3. **Guarantee Scheme**: The State Government guarantees the repayment of principal.
4. **Issuing bonds and debentures** and resorting to borrowings from the RBI.
5. **Refinancing facilities**: Obtaining refinancing facilities from the IDBI.

6. **Public Deposits**: Accepting public deposits from the public for a period not less than one year and not exceeding its paid-up share capital.

SFCs (Amendment) Act, 2000

To provide greater functional autonomy and operational flexibility to SFCs Government brought some amendments to the SFCs Act of 1956 in the year 2000. The main features of the amended Act are as follows.

1. **Share capital.** Share capital held by IDBI was transferred to SIDBI. The authorised capital of SFC fixed by state governments was increased from Rs. 50 lakhs to Rs. 500 crores provisions was made to increase up to Rs.1000 crores if the state government is ready to contribute up to 51 percent. It can issue both equity shares and redeemable preference shares. State governments should hold at least 51 percent of shares.
2. **Resources.** The SFCs can raise resources by the issue of bonds and debentures, borrowings from RBI, borrowings from state governments. Upto 30 times of paid up capital and reserve fund with the prior approval of SIDBI. The borrowings from state government/local authority or any other person repayable after 12 months.
3. **Management.** The Chairman and Board of Directors are appointed in consultation with state governments. Managing Director is appointed by state governments. Two directors are appointed by SIDBI, two by state governments, two by other financial institutions, two to four by other shareholders.
4. **Business.** The SFCs are allowed to take up the following business under the amended the Act.
   1. Consultancy and merchant banking services
   2. Acting as trustee for the debenture holders
   3. Leasing, sub-leasing, hire / purchase
   4. Factoring
   5. Export related credit and services

6. Money market related activities
7. Setting up of Mutual Funds and Asset Management Companies
8. Promotion and conduct of companies, subsidiaries. societies, trusts etc.

5. Limit of accommodation. The limit for accommodation of loan prior to amendment to an industrial concern was not to exceed Rs.150 lakhs. In case of corporation or co-operative society it was Rs. 90 lakhs. These limits have been raised to Rs. 5 crores and Rs. 2 crores respectively. For corporations SIDBI permitted to increase to Rs.10 crores.

6. Prohibited assistance. The industrial concern whose paid up capital and free reserves exceeded Rs. 3 crores it raised later to Rs.10 crores, and such higher amount not exceeding Rs. 30 crores, as the state government may specify is prohibited to get assistance under SFCs.

STATE INDUSTRIAL DEVELOPMENT CORPORATIONS (SIDCs)

The first SIDC was established in Bihar in 1960 later on in most of the states they were established during 1960s and 1970s. They are wholly owned by the respective state governments. Some of them are set up under State Acts as statutory autonomous corporation (Maharashtra and Gujarat), other corporations established by other state governments they are either private or public limited companies under the Companies Act, 1956. There are about 28 SIDCs/SIICs. The main aim of these SIDCs is to promote rapid industrialization and to bring about balanced regional development by assisting backward areas. They give assistance to medium, large, and small units.

Functions

The main functions of SIDCs are:

1. To provide risk capital in the form of equity and seed capital.
2. To give term loans, guarantees, and lease finance.

3. To administer incentive schemes of the central and state governments.
4. To conduct surveys on industrial potential to identify project ideas, prepare feasibility reports, and select and train entrepreneurs.
5. To develop industrial areas, plots, sheds, and estates.
6. To set up industrial projects in the joint sector like partnership with private entrepreneurs or as wholly-owned subsidiaries.

MUTUAL FUNDS IN INDIA

The concept of Mutual Funds was started with Unit Schemes of Unit Trust of India in 1964 in India. The term mutual funds came into prominence only in 1987 when leading public sector banks (PSBs) like State Bank of India and Canara Bank set up their mutual funds, followed by Life Insurance Corporation of India in 1989. From the year 1993 the mutual funds were allowed to start under private sector also. Now we have around 40 mutual fund companies under public, private and joint ventures with foreign companies. There are around 196 mutual fund schemes, and the amount of assets under their management was Rs. 47,000 crores in 1993, Rs. 80,590 crores in March 31, 2003 and it went up to Rs, 2,17,707 crores by 31, March 2006.

In case of large number of small investors, who do not have the knowledge of investing funds in the corporate securities, there is an option of giving savings to the mutual fund companies under different schemes, by purchasing the unit under that scheme. They can select the schemes offered by the mutual fund companies on the basis of risks and expectations of the investors. The mutual fund companies have experts or the professionals who invest the funds as per the scheme. These professionals are in the know of the timing of investments, when to buy or sell securities, the volume of buying / selling, where to buy, in which companies, sectors, securities to be invested etc. with such expertise of the markets, the professionals invest funds/savings collected in the market and sell when the market is profitable. These profits are distributed to the investors under the scheme in the proportion of number of units purchased.

Meaning

A Mutual Fund is a trust that pools the savings of a number of investors who share a common financial goal. The money thus collected is then invested in capital market instruments such as equities, debentures and other securities. The income earned through these investments and the capital appreciation reaslised are shared by its unit holders in proportion to the number of units owned by them.

The Mutual Fund is a trust at law: it is a special type of managed, pooled portfolio financial company or financial service organization that sells shares/units /stocks in itself, to the public to obtain its resources, and it invests the savings so mobilized or pooled in a large, diversified, and sound portfolio of equity shares, bonds and money market instruments.

Mutual fund is a mechanism for pooling the resources by issuing units to the investors and investing funds in securities in accordance with the objectives as disclosed in offer document. Investments in securities are spread across a wide cross-section of industries and sectors and thus the risk is reduced. Diversification reduces the risk because all stocks may not move in the same direction and in the same proportion at the same time. Mutual funds issue units to the investors in accordance with quantum of money invested by them. Investors of mutual funds are known as unit holders. The profits or losses are shared by the investors in proportion to their investments.

The mutual funds normally come out with a number of schemes with different investment objectives which are launched from time to time. Before starting its operations, i.e. collecting funds from the public, a mutual fund is required to register itself with the Securities and Exchange Board of India (SEBI) which regulates securities markets.

Operations of Mutual Funds

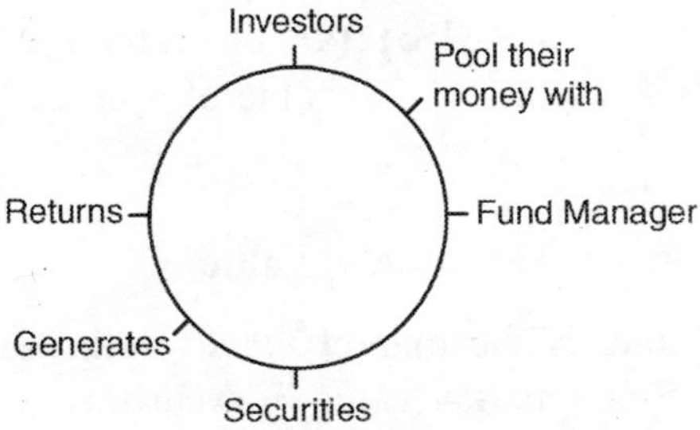

Organization of Mutual Fund Companies in India

The organization of mutual funds involves five constituents or special bodies. They are:

1. The Sponsor/s.
2. The Board or Trustees / Trust company
3. The Asset Management Company (AMC)
4. The Custodian and
5. The Unit holders.

A mutual fund is set up in the form of a trust, which has sponsor, trustees, Asset Management Company (AMC) and custodian. The trust is established by a sponsor or more than one sponsor who is like a promoter of a company. The trustees of the mutual fund hold its property for the benefit of the unit holders. Asset Management Company (AMC) approved by SEBI manages the funds by making investments in various types of securities. Custodian, who is registered with SEBI, holds the securities of various schemes of the fund in its custody. The trustees are vested with the general power of superintendence and direction over AMC. They monitor the performance and compliance of SEBI Regulations by the mutual fund.

SEBI Regulations require that at least two-thirds of the directors of trustee company or board of trustees must be independent i.e. they should not be associated with the sponsors besides 50% of the directors of AMC must be independent. All mutual funds are required to be registered with SEBI before they launch any scheme. However, Unit Trust of India (UTI) is not registered with SEBI (as on January 15, 2002). The performance of a particular scheme of a mutual fund is denoted by Net Asset Value (NAV).

Computation of Net Assets Value

Net Asset Value is the market value of the securities held by the scheme. Since market value of securities changes every day, NAV of a scheme also varies on day-to-day basis. The NAV per unit is the market value of securities of a scheme divided by the total number of units of the scheme on any particular date. For example, if the market value of securities of a mutual fund scheme is Rs 200 crores and the mutual fund has issued 10 crore units of Rs. 10 each to the investors, then the NAV per unit of the fund is Rs. 20. NAV is required to be disclosed by the mutual funds on a regular—daily or weekly basis—depending on the type of scheme.

Classification of Types of Schemes

1. A mutual fund scheme can be classified into open-ended scheme or close-ended scheme depending on its maturity period.

An ***open-ended scheme*** is one that is available for subscription and repurchase on a continuous basis. These schemes do not have a fixed maturity period. Investors can conveniently buy and sell units at Net Asset Value (NAV) related prices which are declared on a daily basis. Liquidity is the key feature of open-ended schemes.

A ***close-ended scheme*** has a stipulated maturity period e.g. 5-7 years. The fund is open for subscription only during a specified period at the time of launch of the scheme. Investors can invest in the scheme at the time of the initial public issue and thereafter they can buy or sell the units of the scheme on the stock exchanges where the units are listed. In order to provide an exit route to the investors, some close-ended funds give an option of selling back the units to the mutual fund through periodic repurchase at NAV related prices. SEBI Regulations stipulate that at least one of the two exit routes is provided to the investor i.e. either repurchase facility or through listing on stock exchanges. These mutual fund schemes disclose NAV generally on weekly basis.

Differences between open-ended and close-ended schemes

The following are the differences:

1. The close-ended schemes are open to the public for a limited period, whereas the open-ended schemes are always open to be subscribed all the time.
2. Close-ended schemes will have a definite period of life. But the open-ended schemes are transacted in the company.
3. Close-ended schemes are transacted at stock exchanges, whereas open-ended schemes are transacted (bought and sold) in the company.
4. Close-ended schemes are terminated at the end of the specified period. Open-ended schemes can be terminated only if the total number of units outstanding after repurchase fall below 50 percent of the original number of units.

2. **A scheme can also be classified** as growth scheme, income scheme, or balanced scheme considering its investment objective. Such schemes may be open-ended or close-ended as described earlier. Such schemes may be classified mainly as follows:

   a. ***Growth funds.*** The aim of growth funds is to provide capital appreciation over the medium- to long-term. Such schemes normally invest a major part of their corpus in equities. Such funds have comparatively high risks. These schemes provide different options to the investors like dividend option, capital appreciation, etc. and the investors may choose an option depending on their preferences. The investors must indicate the option in the application form. The mutual funds also allow the investors to change the options at a later date. Growth schemes are good for investors that have a long-term outlook seeking appreciation over a period of time.

b. ***Income funds.*** The aim of income funds is to provide regular and steady income to investors. Such schemes generally invest in fixed income securities such as bonds, corporate debentures, government securities and money market instruments. Such funds are less risky as compared to equity schemes. These funds are not affected because of fluctuations in equity markets. However, opportunities of capital appreciation are also limited in such funds. The NAV of such funds are affected because of change in interest rates in the country. If the interest rates fall, NAVs of such funds are likely to increase in the short run and vice versa. However, long-term investors may not bother about these fluctuations.

c. ***Balanced funds.*** The aim of balanced funds is to provide both growth and regular income as such schemes invest both in equities and fixed income securities in the proportion indicated in their offer documents. These are appropriate for investors looking for moderate growth. They generally invest 40-60% in equity and debt instruments. These funds are also affected by fluctuations in share prices in the stock markets. However, NAVs of such funds are likely to be less volatile as compared to pure equity funds. There are also exchange traded index funds launched by the mutual funds which are traded on the stock exchanges.

d. ***Money Market Mutual Funds (MMMFs).*** These funds are also income funds and their aim is to provide easy liquidity, preservation of capital and moderate income. These schemes invest exclusively in safer short-term instruments such as treasury bills, certificates of deposit, commercial paper and inter-bank call money, government securities, etc. Returns on these schemes fluctuate much less as compared to other funds. These funds are appropriate for corporate and individual investors as a means to park their surplus funds for short periods.

e. ***Indexed funds***. These funds invest exclusively in government securities. Government securities have no default risk. NAVs of these schemes also fluctuate due to change in interest rates and other economic factors as is the case with income or debt oriented schemes. Index funds replicate the portfolio of a particular index such as the BSE Sensitive index, S&P NSE 50 index (Nifty), etc. These schemes invest in the securities in the same weightage comprising index. NAVs of such schemes would rise or fall in accordance with the rise or fall in the index, though not exactly by the same percentage due to some factors known as "tracking error" in technical terms. Necessary disclosures in this regard are made in the offer document of the mutual fund scheme.

f. ***Sector Scheme.*** These are the funds/schemes which invest in the securities of only those sectors or industries as specified in the offer documents. e.g. pharmaceuticals, software, fast moving consumer Goods (FMCG), petroleum stocks, etc. The returns in these funds are dependent on the performance of the respective sectors/industries. While these funds may give higher returns, they are more risky as compared to diversified funds. Investors need to keep a watch on the performance of those sectors/industries and must exit at an appropriate time besides seeking expert advice.

g. ***Tax Saving Schemes***. These schemes offer tax rebates to the investors under specific provisions of the Income Tax Act, 1961 as the Government offers tax incentives for investment in specified avenues. e.g. Equity Linked Savings Schemes (ELSS). Pension schemes launched by the mutual funds also offer tax benefits. These schemes are growth oriented and invest predominantly in equities. Their growth opportunities and risks associated are like any equity-oriented scheme.

h. ***Load Fund***. A Load Fund is one that charges a percentage of NAV for entry or exit. ie, each time one buys or sells units in the fund, a charge will be payable. This charge is used by the mutual fund for marketing and distribution expenses. Suppose the NAV per unit is Rs.10 and entry as well as exit load charged is 1%, then the investors who buy would be required to pay Rs.10.10 and those who offer their units for repurchase to the mutual fund will get only Rs.9.90 per unit. The investors should take the loads into consideration while making investment as these affect their yields/returns. However, the investors should also consider the performance track record and service standards of the mutual fund which are more important. Efficient funds may give higher returns in spite of loads.

i. ***No-load fund***. A no-load fund is one that does not charge for entry or exit. It means the investors can enter the fund/scheme at NAV and no additional charges are payable on purchase or sale of units. The price or NAV a unit holder is charged while investing in an open-ended scheme is called sales price. It may include sales load, if applicable.

Repurchase or redemption price is the price or NAV at which an open-ended scheme purchases or redeems its units from the unit holders. It may include exit load, if applicable.

How to invest in a scheme of a mutual fund?

Mutual funds normally come out with an advertisement in newspapers publishing the date of launch of the new schemes. Investors can also contact the agents and distributors of mutual funds who are spread all over the country for necessary information and application forms. Forms can be deposited with mutual funds through the agents and distributors who provide such services. Nowadays, the post-offices and banks also distribute the units of mutual funds. However, the investors may note that the mutual funds schemes being marketed by banks and post-offices should not be taken as their own schemes and no assurance of returns is given by them. The only role of banks and post-offices is to help in distribution of mutual funds schemes to the investors. Investors should not be carried away by commission/gifts given by agents/distributors for investing in a particular scheme. On the other hand they must consider the track record of the mutual fund and should take objective decisions.

Functions of Mutual Funds

Functions
1. Buying and selling of securities on behalf of its unit holders. 2. It reduces the risks of investment 3. Pooled in a large and diversified and sound portfolio. 4. It gives investors a share in its total funds. 5. No voting rights 6. Benefit of professional management of funds 7. Accessibility to small investors in profitable avenues in capital and money markets.

1. The basic function of mutual fund companies is buying and selling securities on behalf of its unit holders.
2. It enables small investors to hold a share in a large and diversified portfolio of assets which reduces the risks of investment.

3. The savings so mobilized are pooled in a large, diversified, and sound portfolio of equity, bonds, securities etc.
4. Investors in the mutual funds are given the share in its total funds which is evidenced by the unit certificates.
5. Mutual fund holders do not have any voting rights.
6. It is possible for small investors to have the benefit of professional management of portfolio, which, in turn, helps them to earn a relatively higher rate of return.
7. It helps the small investors who do not have adequate time, knowledge, expertise, experience, and resources for directly accessing profitable avenues in capital and money markets.

Benefits of Mutual Funds

Benefits of Mutual Funds

1. Professional management
2. Diversification of funds
3. Economies of scale of operation
4. Spread of risk
5. Liquidity
6. Freedom from housekeeping
7. Choice of schemes
8. Well regulated

The following are the benefits of Mutual Funds:

1. ***Professional Management*: The schemes under mutual funds are managed by the professionals who have expert knowledge of the capital market.
2. ***Diversification of Funds*: The funds (money) collected under the schemes are invested by the fund managers in a diversified portfolio of equity, bonds, debentures of the large and good performing companies from various sectors like manufacturing, IT, BT, pharmaceuticals, cement, steel etc.
3. ***Economies of scale of operation:*** A mutual fund company pools the funds of many small investors under the scheme and invested by one AMC. Since it is managed by one

AMC the cost of administration and other expenses like brokerage and transaction cost will be less.

4. ***Spread of risk:*** Under mutual fund companies the risk is spread among all the investors by investing the funds collected under scheme in diversified securities. Hence in the case of any market crash or for any reason if the loss is incurred it is spread among all the unit holders of the scheme.
5. ***Liquidity:*** The money invested under mutual funds is highly liquid. Hence whenever the securities rates boom up (bulls operating in the market) the fund managers will sell the securities and buy the securities when the bears are operating in the market. Till then they hold the securities.
6. ***Freedom from housekeeping:*** The investors after purchasing the units under the schemes need not bother about buying/selling, market behaviour, safety of the money, liquidity etc. all these are taken care by the mutual fund companies.
7. ***Choice of schemes:*** The advantage of the mutual fund companies is that the investor can invest his money in any of the schemes offered by the company. In MFs there are good number of schemes, the investors on the basis of their choice of risk bearing capacity can invest in the scheme.
8. ***Well regulated:*** The mutual fund companies are well regulated by SEBI. There is transparency in the investments; hence the investor can verify the money invested under the scheme.

In early 1990s, the government allowed public sector banks and institutions to set up mutual funds. In the year 1992, Securities and Exchange Board of India (SEBI) Act was passed. The objectives of SEBI are to protect the interest of investors in securities and to promote the development of and to regulate the securities market.

As far as mutual funds are concerned, SEBI formulates policies and regulates the mutual funds to protect the interest of the investors. SEBI notified regulations for the mutual funds in the year 1993. Thereafter, mutual funds sponsored by private sector entities were allowed to enter the capital market. The regulations were fully revised in 1996 and have been amended thereafter from time to time. SEBI has also issues guidelines to the mutual funds from time to time to protect the interests of investors.

All mutual funds whether promoted by public sector or private sector entities including those promoted by foreign entities are governed by the same set of Regulations. There is no distinction in regulatory requirements for these mutual funds and all are subject to monitoring and inspection by SEBI. The risks associated with the schemes launched by the mutual funds sponsored by these entities are of similar type. It may be mentioned here that Unit Trust of India (UTI), the oldest and the largest MF in India which was established in 1964, is not registered with SEBI as a mutual fund (as on January 15, 2002).

Growth in Assets Under Management (Rs. In crores)

The growth of mutual fund industry can be broadly put into four phases according to the development of the sector. Each phase is briefly described as under.

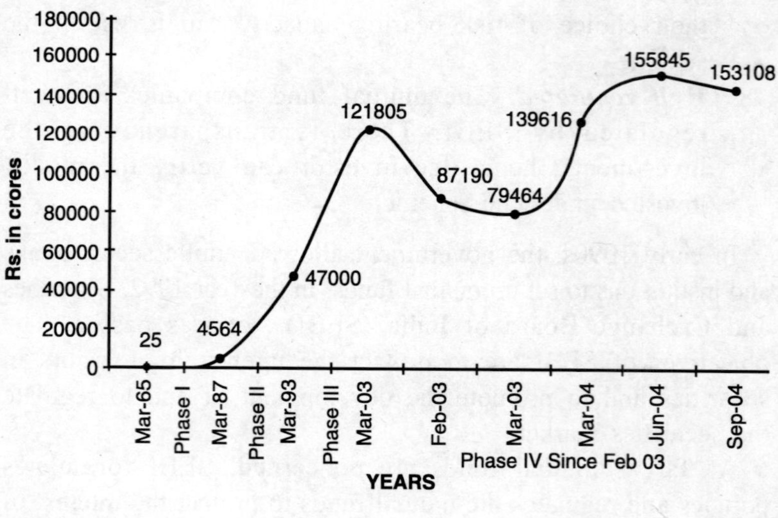

First Phase : 1964-87

Unit Trust of India (UTI) was established on 1963 by an Act of Parliament. It was set up by the Reserve Bank of India and functioned under the regulatory and administrative control of the Reserve Bank of India. In 1978 UTI was de-linked from the RBI and the Industrial Development Bank of India (IDBI) took over the regulatory and administrative control in place of RBI. The first scheme launched by UTI was Unit Scheme 1964. At the end of 1988 UTI had Rs. 6,700 crores of assets under management

Second Phase : 1987-1993 (Entry of Public Sector Funds)

SBI Mutual Fund was the first followed by Canbank Mutual Fund (Dec, 87), Punjab National Bank Mutual Fund (Aug, 89), Indian Bank Mutual Fund (Nov, 89), Bank of India (June, 90), Bank of Baroda Mutual Fund (Oct, 92), LIC in 1989 and GIC in 1990. The end of 1993 marked Rs. 47,004 crores as assets under management.

Third Phase : 1993-2003 (Entry of Private Sector Funds)

With the entry of private sector funds in 1993, a new era started in the Indian mutual fund industry, giving the Indian investors a wider choice of fund companies. Also, 1993 was the year in which the first Mutual Fund Regulations came into being, under which all mutual funds, except UTI were to be registered and governed. The 1993 SEBI (Mutual Fund) Regulations were substituted by a more comprehensive and revised Mutual Fund Regulations in 1996. The industry now functions under the SEBI (Mutual Fund) Regulations 1996. The number of mutual fund houses went on increasing, with many foreign players setting up funds in India and also the industry has witnessed several mergers and acquisitions. As at the end of January 2003, there were 33 mutual funds with total assets of Rs. 1,21,805 crores. The Unit Trust of India with Rs. 44,541 crores of assets under management was way ahead of other mutual funds.

Fourth Phase : Since February 2003

This phase had bitter experience for UTI. It was bifurcated into two separate entities. One is the Specified Undertaking of the Unit Trust of India with AUM of Rs. 29,835 crores (as on January 2003). The Specified Undertaking of Unit Trust of India, functioning under an administrator and under the rules framed by Government of India, does not come under the purview of the Mutual Fund Regulations.The second is the UTI Mutual Fund Ltd, sponsored by SBI, PNB, BOB and LIC. It is registered with SEBI and functions under the Mutual Fund Regulations. With the bifurcation of the erstwhile UTI which had in March 2000 more than Rs.76,000 crores of AUM and with the setting up of a UTI Mutual Fund, conforming to the SEBI Mutual Fund Regulations, and with recent mergers taking place among different private sector funds, the mutual fund industry has entered its current phase of consolidation and growth. As at the end of September, 2004, there were 29 funds, with assets of Rs. 1,53,108 crores under 421 schemes.

UNIT TRUST OF INDIA

Unit Trust of India was the first mutual fund set up in India in the year 1964 under UTI Act of 1963. UTI first pioneered the concept of pooled investment management in India. The basic objective of the establishment of UTI was, to "**encourage investment and participation in the income, profits and gains accruing to the corporation from the acquisition, holding, management and disposal of securities.**" It was established to channelise investors' savings towards corporate and other securities and enable them to share in the widening industrial prosperity in the country.

The initial capital of US 64 was fixed at 5 crores and it was contributed by RBI, LIC, SBI and its subsidiaries and other scheduled banks including a few foreign banks. It can be irredeemable at the discretion of UTI at such values as may be decided by GOI. Accordingly the share of RBI has transferred to IDBI.

Organisation of UTI: UTI is managed and controlled by a Board of Trustees, which is headed by a Chairman appointed by GOI. Four trustees and the Executive Trustee are appointed by IDBI. Remaining trustees are nominated by other contributors to the initial capital. Trust operates as an autonomous body expected to operate on commercial principles with due regard to the interest of unit holders.

Mobilization of Savings

Commencing from US 64 the trust introduced a large number of Unit Schemes to mobilize the savings of different classes of investors. These schemes are tailored to the needs different categories of investors. It has two categories of schemes:

1. Open-ended schemes
2. Close-ended schemes and

Other schemes like Growth schemes, Incomes schemes and so on. Monthly Income US, Growing Income, Growing monthly income, Deferred income, Growth schemes, Income-cum-growth schemes, Off shore funds, Venture capital. Most of the schemes except US 64 have come under the purview of SEBI. As on June 30, 1998, 79 US were in operation consisting of 28 open-ended and 51 close-ended schemes.

Progress of Resource Mobilization (Assets) by UTI (in crores)

Year	Total Assets/Liabilities
1964-74	176
1984-85	2298
1994-95	63006
1997-98	68386
1998-99	72836
1999-00	81607
2000-01	80437
2001-02	66271

The savings mobilized by the Unit Trust of India during the year 1964-74 was Rs. 176 crores, which increased to Rs. 81,607 crores by the year 1999-2000. During the year 1998 there were negative reserves because of crisis in US 64 schemes which affected the resource mobilization. Later after the bifurcation of UTI into UTI I and UTI II, US 64 scheme and Monthly income schemes of UTI were brought under UTI I and rest of the schemes under UTI II. The UTI I started regaining by the year 2003 onwards.

Diversification of activities of UTI

To diversify its activities UTI has established the following subsidiaries:

1. The UTI Bank Ltd., 1994.
2. UTI Investor Services Ltd.
3. UTI Securities Exchange Ltd., 1997.
4. UTI Investment Advisory Services.
5. UTI Institute of Capital Markets.

US 64 Crises

Since its inception in 1964 US 64 was doing very well by attracting the confidence of the public through its consistent growth. Till September 1998 investors felt that investment in US 64 was sound and safe. At the end of September 1998 a report of US 64 appeared in the newspapers that the balance sheet of July 1998 was showing negative reserves of Rs. 1,098 crores. Hence the investors realized that the selling price of the US 64 was more than the actual NAV and started selling the units. There was mad rush for the selling of the units and the sensex lost over 220 points. The RBI came to the rescue of UTI and managed the situation and also constituted a committee under the chairmanship of Shri Deepak Parekh to investigate the reasons for the negative reserves and suggest measures to be taken to retain the investors' confidence and to strengthen the US 64 Scheme.

Causes of Negative Reserves

The following are the causes identified by the Committee for negative reserves.

1. ***Changed Investment Policy***. The debt equity composition from 1986 was 79: 21 which changed to 37:63 by the year 1998. In addition to it the UTI participated in the purchase of the share of PSUs disinvestment programme of Government of India and also indiscriminate buying of the shares of low quality through Initial Public Offer.
2. ***Pricing policy of the Units***. The UTI was not buying and selling units on the basis of NAV. UTI was deciding the price by itself and following the trend pricing which doesn't had any relationship with NAV. The policy of following a stable price irrespective of market fluctuations has contributed to the investor perception that safety of capital was assured to the investors. This eroded the profits of UTI.
3. ***Dividend Distribution Policy***. The UTI followed the policy of declaring dividends at gradually increasing rates since the beginning of the scheme. This dividend policy protected the interests of the investors by declaring high dividends than the actual value.

Suggestions of the Committee

1. The Committee suggested the IDBI, LIC, SBI, and its subsidiaries and other institutions who are contributors of initial capital of the US 64 scheme to inject Rs. 500 crores into the corpus of the scheme as an additional share.
2. The Committee suggested the GOI to subscribe to Special Unit Scheme 99 (SUS 99) by transferring the PSUs stocks held by US 64 to the extent of loss (Rs. 4,800 crores) in the depreciation of book values of PSUs stock.
3. Investment in US 64 given tax exemptions.
4. The committee suggested that commercial banks be encouraged to contribute Rs. 2,500 crores to the corpus

of a new equity related scheme to be promoted by the UTI.

5. UTI Act should be amended to increase the number of Board of Trustees, provision to set up Asset Management Company (AMC) to manage the funds.
6. The Committee suggested to appoint independent fund managers for each scheme and inter-scheme transfers of investments should be at market-determined prices.
7. US 64 should become a NAV driven scheme.

LIFE INSURANCE CORPORATION OF INDIA

The insurance industry has both economic and social responsibility and relevance. It provides social security and promotes individual welfare. It reduces risk and helps to raise productivity in economy. Thus the insurance companies are financial intermediaries as they collect and invest large amount of premiums. They offer protection to the investors, so insurance business consists of spreading of risks over time and sharing them between persons and organizations.

Historical Perspective of Insurance in India

The Life Insurance business in India started in the year 1818 with the establishment of the Oriental Life Insurance Company in Calcutta. It was started to provide life insurance for Britishers. At that time a higher premium was charged for the Indian lives than the non-Indian lives as Indian lives were considered more risky for life coverage.

In 1850 the first general insurance company by name Triton Insurance Co. was established. Bombay Mutual Life Insurance Society started its business in 1870. This was the first company which charged the same premium for both Indian and non-Indian lives. Oriental Assurance Co. was established in 1880 at that time overseas companies had major role in setting up the insurance company in India.

After 19th century there was gradual change in insurance business and insurance regulation formally began in India with the passing of LIC Act of 1912 and the Provident Fund Act of 1912. Several frauds during 1920's and 1930's sullied insurance business in India. By 1938 there were 176 companies. The first comprehensive legislation was introduced with the Insurance Act of 1938 that provided strict state control over insurance business.

The insurance business grew at a faster pace after independence. Indian companies strengthened their hold on this business, but despite the growth that was witnessed, insurance remained an urban phenomenon. The Government of India in 1956 brought together over 240 private life insurers and provident societies under one nationalized monopoly corporation i.e., Life Insurance Corporation of India. Nationalization was justified on the grounds that it would create much needed funds for rapid industrialization.

Development of Life Insurance Corporation

LIC of India was established in September 1956 to spread the message of Life Insurance in the country and mobilize people's savings for nation building activities. LIC with its central office in Mumbai and seven zonal offices at Mumbai, Calcutta, Delhi, Chennai, Hyderabad, Kanpur, and Bhopal operates through 100 divisional offices in important cities and 2,048 branch offices, LIC has 5.59 lakh active agents spread over the country by the year 2004. The Corporation also transacts business abroad and has offices in Fiji, Mauritius, and U.K. etc. LIC is associated with Joint Venture abroad in the field of insurance, namely:

1. Ken-India Assurance Co. Ltd, Nairobi.
2. United Oriental Assurance Co. Ltd. Kuala Lumpur.
3. Life Insurance Corporation (International) E.C., Bahrain.

It has also entered into an agreement with Sun Life (UK) for marketing unit linked life insurance and pension policies in U.K.

LIC of India is the biggest life insurance company in India. For the past 4 decades.

Objectives of LIC of India

The Life Insurance Corporation of India was established with the following objectives:

1. Spread life insurance widely and in particular to the rural areas, to the socially and economically backward classes with a view to reaching all insurable persons in the country and providing them adequate financial cover against death at a reasonable cost.
2. Maximize mobilization of people's savings by making insurance linked savings adequately attractive.
3. Bear in mind, in the investment of funds, the primary obligation is to its policy holders, whose money it holds best advantage of the investors as well as the community as a whole, keeping in view national priorities and obligations of attractive return.
4. Conduct business with utmost economy and with the full realization that the money belong to the policy holders.
5. Act as trustees of the insured public in their individual and collective capacities.
6. Meet the various life insurance needs of the community that would arise in the changing social and economic environment.
7. Involve all people working in the Corporation to the best of their capability in furthering the interest of the insured public by providing efficient service with courtesy.

Share of Insurance Sector in Household Financial Savings

The share of insurance sector in household financial savings has increased from 7.6% during 1980's to 10.1% during 1990's and 12% in 2000-01. The share of insurance sector in GDP has been about 0.6% in the all these years.

Share of Insurance Sector In Household Financial Savings

	1980's	1990's	2000-01
1) Share of Insurance sector in Household Financial Savings	7.6%	10.1%	12%
2) The Share of Insurance sector in GDP	7.6%	0.6%	0.6%

The share of insurance sector in household financial savings considerably increased from 1980's i.e. 7.6 percent to 12% in 2000-01 that means this insurance sector is successful in creating habit of savings among the people even though it has to compete with the other saving institutions like banks, mutual funds, pension funds, etc. to attract household savings.

Savings of Household Sector

Savings of the household sector in the LIC investment media as % Total Household savings in the form of financial assets.

1956-57	1960-61	1965-66	1970-71	1988-89	1995-96	2000-01
5.5%	12.3%	8%	9.8%	7%	10.8%	12%

The following Table gives us a good idea about the growing importance of LIC as a financial intermediary. Its new as well as outstanding business has grown rapidly since 1950 onwards.

Insurance penetration and Insurance Density

From the above information it could be concluded that the Indian insurance business has remained underdeveloped and this has been attributed to the state monopoly and lack of aggressive marketing and insurance policies.

The real cause for the so called underdeveloped nature of the formal organized insurance services is to be sought in the social security which has been provided to the individuals by families, communities and villages in India over thousands of

Insurance Penetration and Insurance Density

Country	Insurance penetration (IP)			Insurance Density (Per capita insurance premium)		
	Non-life%	Life %	Total %	Non-life $	Life $	Total $
1. USA	4.28	4.48	8.76	1541	1611	3152
2. Brazil	1.75	.36	2.11	63	13	76
3. Mexico	.85	.86	1.72	50	51	101
4. U.K	3.07	12.71	15.78	731	3028	3759
5. Russia	1.29	1.13	2.42	22	19	41
6. Japan	2.22	8.70	10.92	808	3165	3973
7. China	.67	1.12	1.79	6	9	15
8. Malaysia	1.59	2.13	3.72	65	86	151
9. Indonesia	.64	.54	1.18	5	4	9
10. South Africa	2.83	14.04	16.86	79	393	472
11. Kenya	1.91	.72	2.63	6	2	8
12. India	.55	1.77	2.32	2	8	10

years is less and the occupational pattern of jobs and social organizations had nearly eliminated the necessity for the formal insurance, which is reflected in the low values of IP, ID and such other indicators of insurance coverage.

Summary Of Life Insurance Business In India (Rs. In crore)

Year	Total Premium	Pvt. Sector	% of Pvt. Sector	Public Sector	% of Public Sector	Total Invest-ments	Of which in Govt. & Other Securities	Other than Approved Invest-ments.
2000-01	36070	7	0.02	36063	99.98	139926	103058	36868
2001-02	50094	273	0.54	49821	99.46	173370	132177	16521
2002-03	57905	3277	5.66	54628	94.34	213477	166264	47213
2003-04	76707	13577	17.7	63130	82.30	256105	204341	51764

The Table given above shows that LIC's business after the entry of private players. In 2000-01 the business was 99.98% and it decreased to 99.46%, 94.34%, 82.30% in 2001-20, 2002-03, 2003-04 respectively.

Growth of Individual Life Insurance Business in India (amounts in Rs. Crore and numbers in Lakhs)

Year	New Business			Total Business in Force				Total Invest-ments
	No. of policies	Sum Assured	Premium Income	No. of policies	Sum Assured	Premium Income	Life Fund	
1950	4.98	139	-	-	780	41	224	227
1955	7.96	240	-	-	1128	58	300	328
1960	12.5	488	20	75	2176	93	520	527
1965	15.5	789	31	114	4282	175	931	962
1975	20.1	2104	94	196	13248	543	3382	-
1986	38.7	9067	372	298	47906	1885	14406	13936
1995	110	51816	2332	708	294336	12094	72280	68276
1999	169	91214	4956	1014	536451	24207	15404	146364

It is observed from the Table above that the policies in the New Business in 1950 were 4.98 lakhs, it increased to Rs.169.77 lakhs by 1999-2000. The sum assured under new business was Rs.139 crores in 1950 it increased to Rs. 91,214 crores by 1999-2000. And even in Premium Income it was Rs. 20 crores and it increased Rs. 4956 crores by 1999-2000. Whereas the number of policies in total business in 1960 was Rs.74.6 lakhs it increased to Rs.1014 by 1999-2000. And sum assured was Rs. 780 crores in 1950 increased to Rs.5, 36,451 crores by 1999-2000.

Premium Income in total business in 1950 was Rs. 41 crores it increased to Rs. 24,207 crores by 1999-00. And the total investment made by the LIC was Rs. 227 crores in 1950 it increased to Rs.1,46,364 crores by 1999-2000.

Schemes of LIC and their Classifications

LIC offers a basket of schemes to meet the various needs of an individual and his family.

I. Basic Life Insurance Plans

1) Whole Life Assurance Plan
2) Endowment Assurance Plan
3) Jeevan Anand

II. Term Assurance Plans

1) LIC's Anmol Jeevan-I
2) Two-year Temporary Assurance Plan
3) Convertible Term Assurance Plan
4) New Bima Kiran

III. Specific Plans for Children

1) Children's Deferred Endowment Assurance
2) Komal Jeevan
3) Jeevan Kishore
4) Jeevan Balya
5) Jeevan Anurag

IV. Pension Plans

1) Jeevan Akshay –II
2) New Jeevan Dhara
3) New Jeevan Suraksha
4) Jeevan Nidhi

V. Plans for Handicapped

1) Jeevan Aadhar (I.T relief u/s 80DD)
2) Jeevan Dependents
3) Jeevan Vishwas

VI. Other Plans

1) Mortgage Redemption
2) New Jana Raksha
3) Fixed term (marriage)
4) Money Back Plans
5) Jeevan Rekha
6) Jeevan Sathi
7) Jeevan Saral

VII. Unit Linked Plans

1) Bima Plus

VIII. Group Schemes

1) Group term insurance schemes
2) Group insurance scheme in the lie of employee's deposits

IX. Social Security Schemes

1) Jan Shree Bima Yojana
2) Swarna Jayanthi Gram Swarojgar Yojana
3) Shiksha Sahayog Yojana-2001

X. Joint Life Plans

1) Jeevan Sathi

XI. Plans to Cover Housing Loans

1) Mortgage Redemption

Lic's Investment Pattern

From the Table below, it is observed that the investment pattern of LIC in 1987 out of total investments 39.60% was invested in Central Government Securities and it increased to 54.84% in 1997 and it further increased to 65.18% by the end of 2004. And investments in State Government Securities it was 14.02% in the year 1987 and it increased marginally to 14.6% in the year 2004. Insurance companies invest their funds judiciously to achieve the objective of safety, liquidity and rate of return. The insurers have to submit to IRDA their investment policies at the beginning of the year of their operations. They have to maintain solvency in their operations. It's from this perspective that the government and IRDA have mandated the pattern of investment to be followed by all the insurers. The IRDA has issued the exposure and prudential norms to the insurance companies.

Reforms in Insurance sector and Insurance Regulatory Development Authority (IRDA)

The insurance sector in India has gone through significant changes through the process of reforms. The IRDA bill was passed by the Indian Parliament in December 1999. The IRDA became the statutory body in April 2000 and has been framing regulations and registering the private sector insurance companies. The insurance sector was opened up to the private players in August 2000. Consequently some Indian and foreign private companies have entered in the insurance business. There were 24 organizations doing life and general insurance business in India in 2004. In addition there is post-office life insurance business also. It is said that over a period of about 200 years the insurance services sector in India has gone through a full circle from being

Type of Investments	31.03.87	31.03.97	31.03.99	31.03.00	31.03.02	31.03.03	31.03.04
Central Government Security	4675	37330	56185	70533	109938	137276	166939
	39.60	54.84	57.33	59.83	63.41	64.30	65.18
State Government Security	1683	8906	12928	14156	21463	28988	37402
	14.26	13.08	13.19	12.00	12.38	13.58	14.6
Electricity (SEB'S)	2603	8214	10591	11931	13447	14508	14805
	22.05	12.07	10.8	10.12	7.76	6.8	5.78
Housing	1872	10967	14207	15884	19054	19944	20694
	15.86	16.11	14.5	13.47	11.00	9.34	8.08
Water Supply and Sewage	718	2028	2508	2997	4000	4420	7111
(MU + ZP)	6.09	2.98	2.56	2.54	2.31	2.07	2.777
State Road Transport	180	540	671	736	893	1358	1373
Corporation	1.52	.79	.68	.62	5.14	.63	.54
Loans to Industrial Estates	37	45	45	45	45	45	45
	.313	.07	.046	.04	.26	.021	.017
Loans to Sugar	37	37	37	37	37	37	37
Co-operatives	.313	.05	.037	.03	.21	.017	.014
Development Authority	1	1	1	1	1	1	1
Roadways, Port,	-	-	25	85	681	781	1272
Railways			.025	.072	.392	.37	.50
Power Generation	-	-	801	1478	3797	6105	6412
			.82	1.25	2.19	2.86	2.50
Municipality	-	-	4	4	14	14	14
Y			.004	.003	.008	.006	.005
TOTAL	11806	68068	98003	117888	173370	213477	256105

on open competitive market to the Nationalized market, and back to a liberalized market again. This is true in a limited sense only; the difference between then and now is noteworthy. Earlier, the number of companies was truly large, the market was really competitive and there was no presence of the state in the insurance market as an owner. Now, the number of companies is small, the market is oligopolistic in which one operator is a dominant leader, there is a heavy concentration of business in the hands of one or two companies and the state is present in the sector as an owner. The earlier competitive private market has been replaced by the present mixed ownership.

Malhotra Committee Recommendations

In 1993, Malhotra Committee headed by former Finance Secretary and RBI Governor R.N. Malhotra, was formed to evaluate the Indian insurance industry and recommend suggestions for its future direction. The Malhotra Committee was set up with the objective of complementing the reforms initiated in the financial sector. The reforms were aimed at "creating a more efficient and competitive financial system suitable for the requirement of the economy keeping in mind the structural changes currently underway and recognizing that insurance is an important part of the overall financial system where it was necessary to address the need for similar reforms."

In 1994 the committee submitted its report and some key recommendations were:

Structure

- Government's stake in the insurance companies to be brought down to 50%
- Government should take over the holdings of GIC and its subsidiaries so that these subsidiaries can act as independent corporations.
- All the insurance companies should be given greater freedom to operate.

Competition

- Private companies with a minimum paid up capital of rupees one billion should be allowed to enter the industry.
- No company should deal both in life and general insurance through a single entity.
- Foreign companies may be allowed to enter the industry in collaboration with domestic companies.
- Postal Life Insurance should be allowed to operate in the rural market.
- Only one state level life insurance company should be allowed to operate in each state.

Regulatory Body

- The Insurance Act should be changed.
- An Insurance Regulatory Body should by set up.
- Controller of Insurance (currently a part of the finance ministry) should be made independent.

Investments

- Mandatory investments of LIC Life fund in Government securities to be reduced from 75% to 50%.
- GIC and its subsidiaries not to hold more than 5% in any company. (Their current holding to be brought down to this level over a period of time.)

Customer Service

- LIC should pay interest on delays in payments beyond 30 days.
- Insurance companies must be encouraged to set up unit-linked pensions plans.
- Computerization of operations and updating of technology to be carried out in the insurance industry.

The Committee emphasized that in order to improve the customer service and increase the coverage insurance industry should be opened up to competition. But at the same time, the Committee felt the need to exercise caution as any failure on the part of new players could ruin the public confidence in the industry. Hence, it was decided to allow competition in a limited way by stipulating the minimum capital requirement of Rs. 100 crores. The Committee felt the need to provide greater autonomy to insurance companies in order to improve their performance and enable them to act as independent companies with economic motives. For this purpose, it had proposed setting up of an independent regulatory body.

Insurance Regulatory Development Authority Act

Insurance Regulatory Development Authority Act (IRDA) came into existence to regulate, promote and to ensure orderly growth and also to protect the interest of policy holders. Insurance in India is regulated by certain rules and regulations.

1. The IRDA has come out with regulations that cover the registration of insurance companies, rural and social obligations of insurers, advertisements, actuaries, agent licensing, re-insurer, assets-liabilities and solvency margins of insurer and appointed actuaries. Additionally, the guidelines for investments for insurance companies have also been laid out.
2. New insurers are expected to offer quality services to their customer at reasonable cost through the application of information technology. In turn, this would generate substantial funds for infrastructural development. However these reforms would also lead to several dilemmas for regulations. The Malhotra Committee had recommended that when private insurers are allowed, it should be done on a selective basis. They should be required to float an Indian company for the purpose, preferably a joint venture with an Indian partner.
3. One of the recommendations was that GIC and LIC

upgrade their technology, re-organize themselves on more efficient lines and operate as board-run enterprises. Even though adequate time was available with both the organizations for re-structuring, there are no clear indications as how successful they have been.

4. The Indian corporate has to assume responsibility for all practical purposes, taking lead and responsibility from their foreign joint venture (JV) partner. Thus JVs are expected to last for a long time since insurance contracts are of long-term in nature. Every regulation has long-term implications. Although there is a advisory committee to approve the regulations, the process of consultation needs to be expanded and widened. Hopefully, wider consultations would be resorted before additional proposed norms are notified.
5. A significant addition in regulatory legislation was the allocation to the regulators of a role in the development of insurance industry. No one is clear where this change was intended to convert nature of regulators' role or will the regulator opt to work towards liberal regulations that would not aim to hold back the insurance companies unnecessarily while coercing them to disclose their affairs including periodical valuations conducted by qualified actuaries.
6. This approach would reflect the philosophy that regulators' intervention would be more reflected in monitoring the operations of insurance companies rather an intrusive type of role. A regulator also has to guard against pressure in the initial stages of the regulatory functioning and to enlarge its role and end up as a super-insurer. This certainly would not have been the intention of the government while opening up of insurance sector for the development and growth, service to customer and nation.
7. Again, large funds are under the custody of the insurer and do get invested to produce the additional returns. The management of these funds is important to the insurer, insured and the economy. Appropriate regulation to channel

the funds flow as to target the developmental areas of the economy may contribute to the overall economic development of the country.

8. The regulators would encourage insurers to concentrate on insurance education so as to make customer and public at large aware of insurance products and other details.
9. Even after liberalization, the influence of government on insurance industry can be felt indirectly through implementation of macro-economic policies and directly through ownership. The relationship between Government and Regulator is going to be crucial for the success of reforms.

Present Players in Insurance Industry in India

Public sector		Private sector	
LIFE	GENERAL	LIFE	GENERAL
1) LIC 2) Post Office Insurance	1) GIC and Its 4 subsidiaries: a) Oriental b) United c) National d) New India Assurance	1) ING Vysya 2) HDFC std. Life 3) ICICI Prudential Life 4) SBI Life 5) Om Kotak Life 6) Met Life 7) Allianz Bajaj Life 8) Max New York Life 9) Tata AIG Life 10) AMP Sanmar 11) Birla Sun Life	1) CHNHB Associates 2) ICICI Lombard 3) Bajaj Allianz 4) Tata AIG General. 5) IFFCO Tokyo 6) Royal Sundram 7) Reliance General

Growth of Individual Life Insurance Business in India after IRDA

Year	New Business			Total Business in Force				
	No. of policies	Sum Assured	Premium Income	No. of policies	Sum Assured	Premium Income	Life Fund	Total Invest-ments
2000-01	197	124951	6591	1131	645042	29270	18602	175491
2001-02	233	192575	14844	1258	811011	39917	245039	216883
2002-03	243	179811	10216	1388	956675	48226	289895	265044
2003-04	265	199698	11752	1562	1113734	63130	337986	343129

The above Table shows that after the setting up of the IRDA the number of policies in the New Business in 2000-01 was Rs.196.65 lakhs; it increased to Rs.264.8 lakhs by 2003-2004.

The sum assured under new business was Rs.1,24,951crores in 2000-01 it increased to Rs. 1,99,698.31 crores by 2003-04. Even in Premium Income it was Rs. 6,591crores and it increased to Rs. 11,752.20 crore by 2003-04.

Whereas the number of Policies in Total Business in 2000-01 was Rs. 1,131 lakhs it increased to Rs. 1,562.44 by 2003-04. The sum assured was Rs. 6,45,042 crores in 2000-01 increased to Rs. 11,13,734.91 by 2003-04.

Premium Income in Total Business in 2000-01 was Rs. 29,270 crores it increased to Rs. 63,13,066 Crore by 2003-04. About total investment made by the LIC it was Rs.1,75,491 crore in 2000-01 it increased to Rs.3,43,129 by 2003-04.

The yield on life insurance products has varied between 7.15% and 9.46% during 1990's. The increase in the resources of insurance companies is beneficial particularly for the government because the major part of these resources is invested in government securities. Thus there is a direct link between the insurance market and government security market.

The expansion of insurance industry helps to ease the fiscal constraints on the country's monetary policy by enlarging the pool of institutional investors in the govt. security market, and by enhancing the flexibility of the central Bank (RBI) to widen the maturity profile of the public debt.

The following table gives us a very good idea about the growing importance of LIC as a financial intermediary it's new as well as outstanding business has grown rapidly during 1950 onwards.

Impact of Liberalization on LIC

The insurance industry in India has gone through a sea change since its liberalization from 1999. Private participation has ushered in a breadth of fresh air into what was considered a dull industry undoubtedly. The erstwhile monopoly, the LIC which spanned the length and breadth of the country has done a commendable job in the industry. The liberalization of the insurance sector, brought many new players from private sector—both domestic and foreign competitors—and also banking institutions entered in to the Indian market to compete with the existing monopolistic LIC of India. LIC has been facing intense competition from the new players. With the entry of new players, the insurance market is flooded with many new and innovative products. LIC has remained the market leader even after the liberalization but with the decreasing of its market share. The LIC of India made some functional changes by withdrawing of some schemes and introducing some new products. It also made some operational changes like customer relationship management, computerization of the work, change in work culture, allowing the employees to leave the organization to reduce its workforce, tie-ups with other banks to promote the products and so on. All these changes are due to acceptance of liberalization process in insurance industry.

EXIM BANK OF INDIA

The Export-Import Bank of India was created by an Act of Parliament, the Export-Import Bank of India Act, 1981. The Bank came into existence in 1982, for the purpose of financing, facilitating and promoting foreign trade of India. It is the principal financial institution in the country for co-ordinating and working of institutions engaged in financing exports and imports.

Organization

The Export-Import Bank of India is fully owned by the Government of India and is managed by a Board of Directors with representation from the government, financial institutions, banks, and the business community. The Board of Directors of the EXIM Bank consists of:

a) A chairman and a managing director appointed by the Central Government: provided that the same person may be appointed to function both as chairman and as managing director.

b) One director is nominated by the RBI.
c) One director nominated by the Development Bank.
d) One director is nominated by the Export Credit and Guarantee Corporation Limited.
e) Not more than twelve directors nominated by the central government of whom:
   (i) Five directors are nominated by the central government
   (ii) Not more than three directors are from the schedule banks.
   (iii) Not more than four directors are persons who have special knowledge of, or professional experience in, export or import or both.

Committees

The Board may constitute such committees whether consisting wholly of directors or wholly of other persons or partly of directors and partly of other persons for such purpose or purposes as it may think fit.

Resources of the EXIM Bank

The resources of the EXIM Bank are:

1. Loans by central government.
2. Borrowings and Acceptance of Deposits by EXIM Bank
3. Loans in foreign currency
4. Grants, donations etc., to EXIM Bank.
5. Export development fund.

Functions of the EXIM Bank

The export finance is the main function of EXIM Bank, and also involves a significant extent in other kinds of export promotional activities. Another salient feature is the extensive involvement of developing Indian economy. The EXIM Bank facilitates the following functions:

1. It provides loans and advances by itself or along with any bank or financial institution whether in or outside India for the purpose of export or import.

2. It also carries on and transacts all or any of the following functions relating to export and import business, namely:
   (a) Granting loans and advances to a scheduled bank or any other banks or financial institution by way of refinance of loans and advances granted by it for purposes of export or import.
   (b) Underwriting the issue of stocks, shares, bonds or debentures of any company engaged in export or import.
   (c) Issuing bid bonds or guarantees in or outside India by itself or in participation with any government, bank or financial institution in or outside India.
   (d) Accepting, collecting, discounting, re-discounting, purchasing, selling or negotiating in or outside India, Bills of exchange or promissory notes arising out of transactions relating to export or import and granting of loans and advances in or outside India against such bills or promissory notes.
   (e) Granting, opening, issuing, confirming or endorsing letters of credit and negotiating or collecting bills and other documents drawn thereunder.
   (f) Undertaking any transactions involving a combination of government to government and commercial credit for the purposes of export or import.
   (g) Granting loans and advances outside India for any Indian joint venture.
   (h) Granting loans and advances to any person in India in connection with his equity contribution in any joint venture in any country outside India.
   (i) Financing export or import of machinery and equipment on lease basis.
   (j) Subscribing to, or investing in, or purchasing of stocks, shares, bonds or debentures of any development bank or export-import bank of any country outside India.
   (k) Buying and selling of, or entering into such other dealings in foreign exchange, as may be necessary for the discharge of its functions.

(l) Issuing participation certificates.

(m) Undertaking and financing of research, surveys, techno-economic or any study in connection with the promotion and development of international trade.

(n) Providing technical, administrative and financial assistance of any kind for export or import.

(o) Collecting, compiling and disseminating market and credit information in respect of international trade and so on.

3. It renders services mentioned in the Act for consideration like commission, brokerage, interest, and remuneration or fees as may be agreed upon.
4. It grants any loan or advance or other financial accommodation on the security of its own bonds or debentures.

EXERCISE

Two marks questions

1. What necessitated the establishment of IDBI?
2. What do you mean by Mutual Funds?
3. Mention the constituents of mutual funds organizations.
4. How do you compute Net Assets Value (NAV)?
5. What do you mean by open-ended scheme?
6. What do you mean by close-ended scheme?
7. What do you mean by growth scheme?
8. What do you mean by indexed scheme?
9. What is the objective of income scheme?
10. Mention the basic objective of establishing UTI.

Five marks questions

1. Explain the role and objectives of IDBI.
2. Why SFCs were established in India? Explain their functions.
3. Explain the working of SFCs.
4. Discuss various sources of financial resources of SFCs.
5. Why SIDCs were established?

6. Distinguish between open-ended and close-ended schemes.
7. How do you invest in a scheme of a Mutual Fund?
8. What was the purpose of starting the EXIM Bank in India? Mention its organizational structure.

Fifteen marks questions

1. Explain the structure and functions of IDBI.
2. What are the amendments brought to the SFCs Act during the year SFCs? What are their implications on the working of SFCs.
3. What is a Mutual Fund? What are its benefits? Explain.
4. Why was EXIM Bank established in India? Explain its functions.

Skill Development

1. Prepare the updated list of financial institutions of India.
2. Collect an annual report and journal published by the Karnataka State Financial Corporation and discuss its activities.
3. Prepare a list of schemes of LIC and ICICI Prudential.
4. Prepare a list of income schemes and growth schemes of any mutual fund company.
5. List the popular schemes of UTI.
6. From the leading newspapers prepare a table showing the movement of NAVs of any two income schemes and growth schemes for two weeks and observe the changes in the schemes.

Chapter 4

REGULATORY INSTITUTIONS

OUTLINE

- Regulatory Institutions
  - Need for regulation
- Reserve Bank of India
  - Organizational structure
  - Functions
- Objectives of Monetary Policy
- Techniques of Monetary Control and Monetary Policy
- National Bank for Agriculture and Rural Development
  - Objectives
  - Functions
  - Organization
  - Major activities
- The Securities and Exchange Board of India
  - Constitution and organization
  - Objectives
  - Powers and functions

LEARNING OBJECTIVES

After studying this chapter you should be able to answer:

1. Which are the regulatory institutions in Indian Financial System?
2. What is the need for regulations?
3. What is the role of RBI?
4. What are the functions of RBI?
5. What are the objectives of monetary policies of RBI?
6. What are the techniques of monetary policies?

NABARD

1. What are the objectives and functions of NABARD?
2. How the NABARD is organized? And what are its major activities.

SEBI

1. How SEBI is organized? What are its objectives?
2. What are the powers and functions of SEBI?

REGULATORY INSTITUTIONS

The regulation of financial system is very essential in any country. It is possible if government creates regulatory institutions, authorities and bodies. The efficient functioning of financial institutions, financial services, financial markets and financial instruments is very essential for a country. The effective regulation will reduce the transaction costs, reduce the failures in the system by reducing price level instability, panic situations, crashes etc. in the markets. The government can promote stability through regulation or by setting up institutions that strengthen the financial system.

In India, we have the following regulatory institutions to regulate the activities of financial system. The Finance Ministry has been continuously formulating major policies in the field of financial sector of the country. The regulators are Ministry of Finance, the Company Law Board (CLB), Department of Economic Affairs, Department of Company Affairs, Reserve Bank of India (RBI), Securities and Exchange Board of India (SEBI) and the Insurance Regulatory and Development Authority (IRDA).

Need for Regulation

The following are the needs for regulating the financial system:

1. Government may promote stability through regulation or by setting up institutions that strengthen the financial system.
2. Through the establishment of regulatory institutions the government intervention may possibly promote competition and lower costs.
3. Financial systems are subject to three forms of instability—panics, crashes, and price-level instability. This may lead to market failures and such extremities can be avoided by the government intervention.
4. The regulators will promote the financial system by its efficient supervision. This will widen the length and breadth of the system.
5. The regulators will protect the interests of its stake holders and concentrate more on the day-to-day activities of its constituents.

RESERVE BANK OF INDIA

Reserve Bank of India is the central bank of the country. It is the nerve centre of the Indian financial and monetary system. As an apex institution, it has been guiding, monitoring, regulating, controlling, and promoting the destiny of the IFS since its inception.

Warren hastings, the then Governor of Bengal made an effort to set up a central bank in January 1773 and he recommended the establishment of a "General Bank in Bengal and Bihar". The next attempt was made in 1807-08 when Robert Richards, a member of the Bombay Government submitted a scheme for a "General Bank". John Maynard Keynes submitted a memorandum entitled "Proposals for the establishment of a State Bank in India" in 1931. Keynes proposed that the State Bank was to perform both central banking and commercial banking functions. But this proposal was not implemented due to the outbreak of the First World War.

The first major step was taken in 1921 when the three

Presidency Banks were amalgamated to form the Imperial Bank of India. It was primarily a commercial bank but it also performed certain central banking functions. In 1926, the Hilton Young Commission recommended that the dichotomy and division of responsibility should be put to rest. It suggested the establishment of a central bank called the "Reserve Bank of India". The Gold Standard and Reserve Bank of India Bill was introduced in the Legislative Assembly in January 1927 but it was dropped because of some differences of opinion. The Indian Constitutional Reforms in 1933 made it obligatory that the transfer of responsibility from the British Government in India to Indians was dependent on the establishment of a Reserve Bank—free from political influence. This led to the introduction of a fresh bill in the Indian Legislative Assembly in 1933 and it received the Governor-General's assent on 6 March 1934 and became an Act on 1 April 1935. It started functioning from April 1, 1935 on the terms of RBI Act of 1934. The RBI was constituted as a shareholders' bank with a fully paid-up capital of Rs. 5 crores divided into shares of Rs 100 each. Of these 5 lakh shares, 2200 share were subscribed by the Directors of the Bank and the remaining by the private shareholders. In 1948 under the Reserve Bank (Transfer to Public Ownership) Act it was nationalized and became a State-owned Bank on 1 January 1949.

Organizational structure of RBI

The organizational structure of the RBI consists of the Central Board of Directors and the Local Board of Directors. The Central Board of Directors consists of 20 members consisting of Governor and 4 Deputy Governors. They are appointed by the Government of India for a period of five years. Four directors are nominated by the Central Government, one each from the four local boards situated at Mumbai, Kolkota, Chennai and New Delhi. Ten Directors nominated by the central government are the experts drawn from various fields. They are appointed for four years.

The 20th member of CBD is a government official who is usually the Secretary, Ministry of Finance nominated by the central Government. The final control vests with the Central Board of Directors.

The Local Board of Directors consists of four from Mumbai, Kolkata, Chennai and New Delhi. The local Board of Directors will be assisted by four members each nominated by central government for a term of four years. And these local boards will advise the Central Board of Directors.

A committee of Central Board of Directors consists of Governor, Deputy Governor and Directors as may be present in the meeting.

Role of Reserve Bank of India

1. To maintain monetary stability
2. To maintain financial stability
3. To maintain stable payments system
4. To promote the development of financial infrastructure of markets and systems
5. To ensure that credit allocation should reflect the national economic priorities and societal concerns.
6. To regulate the overall volume of money and credit in the economy

Reserve Bank of India plays the following roles in the Indian financial system.

1. ***To maintain monetary Stability***. The success of any economy depends upon how best the monetary stability in an economy is maintained. Monetary stability refers to stability of price level. This is done by ensuring matching supply and demand for money in an economy. If the supply of money is more it creates inflation in an economy. If the supply of money in an economy is less then it hampers the progress of an economy with the problem of dearth of money for investment opportunities. Similarly if the demand

for money in an economy is more due to the need for more investments, particularly in the development of infrastructure and in other sectors of an economy leads to dearth of funds in an economy. The supply of money and credit creation etc. should match for a balanced growth of an economy with the demand for money. Ensuring adequate supply of money based on the demand will result in rapid growth of economy which will help in delivering welfare gains to the people of the country.

2. ***To maintain Financial Stability***. The financial stability in an economy depends upon the growth and development of financial sector and also its supervision by the Reserve Bank of India. Financial stability refers to various steps taken to ensure that economy does not face financial instability such as a banking crisis or even extreme financial market volatility which can create severe macro economic consequences. This is done by regulating the activities of commercial banks and other institutions by issuing guidelines and also through monetary policy to ensure monetary stability through financial institutions.

3. ***To maintain stable payments system.*** A secure and stable national payments system is necessary for financial stability in any country. RBI, as the central bank of the country, has taken the initiative for providing the infrastructure for such a payment system. The development of the Real Time Gross Settlement (RTGS) system is in line with the need for sound risk management in large value funds transfer systems. In simple terms, what it means is that with the RTGS systems in place, intra-city credit settlements which used to otherwise take 3-4 days for local cheques and 7-8 working days for outstation cheques will be done instantaneously. Since all RTGS payments are irrevocable and unconditional, it will remove the customer's settlement risk. Since all banks' payments are guaranteed by collateral held at RBI, the RTGS system will reduce 'systemic risk'

in the banking system, thereby providing increased integrity and security for all inter-bank transactions. In addition, RTGS contributes in the reduction of settlement in securities and foreign exchange transactions by providing a mechanism for Delivery versus Payment (DvP) or Payment versus Payment (PvP).

4. ***To promote the development of financial infrastructure of markets and systems.*** The role of RBI includes promoting the development of financial infrastructure of markets like all segments of the capital markets—equities, debt, derivatives, fund products—and will cover all market participants including stock exchanges, trading platforms, clearing and settlement systems, payment systems, depositories, issue houses and other intermediaries. It also includes best practices in setting up, maintaining and upgrading securities market infrastructure.
5. ***To ensure that credit allocation should reflect the national economic priorities and societal concerns.*** The RBI will see that the credit allocation by the financial system broadly reflects the national economic priorities and societal concerns. The RBI instructs all commercial banks to ensure priority sector lending, infrastructure lending, subsidized rates of interests, prime lending rates, sub-prime lending rates etc. It also ensures that specialized institutions are established for the development of certain sectors like manufacturing, service, agriculture and so on.
6. ***To regulate the overall volume of money and credit in the economy***. One important role of RBI is to regulate the volume of money and credit in the economy. The regulation of credit and volume of money in an economy is operated by RBI at present through CRR, SLR, bank rate, open market operations etc.

Functions of RBI

The following are the important functions of Reserve Bank of India

Functions of RBI

1. Note Issuing Authority
2. Banker to Government
3. Bankers' Bank
4. Supervising Authority
5. Exchange Control Authority
6. Promoters of the Financial System

1. Note Issuing Authority

The responsibility of RBI is not only to ***put currency into operation*** but also ***to withdraw it from circulation.*** It also exchanges notes and coins from one denomination to another. The RBI issues currency against the security of gold, foreign securities, Special Drawing Rights, government securities, promissory notes etc. It has the sole right to issue currency notes other than one rupee notes or coins, and coins of smaller denominations. The issuing of notes is conducted through its Issue Department. To discharge its currency functions, the RBI has 15 full-fledged issue offices and 2 sub-offices and 4127 currency chests in which the stock of new and re-issuable notes and coins are stored. Out of 4127 chests 17 chests were with the RBI, 2877 with the SBI and its 7 with associates, 791 with the nationalised banks, 423 with treasuries, and 19 with private sector banks.

2. Banker to Government

RBI is a banker to central and state governments. It provides the governments all banking services such as acceptance of deposits, withdrawal of funds by cheques, making payments as well as receipts and collection of payments on behalf of the government, transfer of funds and management of public debt. The bank receives government deposits free of interest, and it is not entitled to any remuneration for the conduct of the ordinary banking business of the government. The deficit or surplus in the central government account with the RBI is managed by the creation and cancellation of ad-hoc Treasury Bills and that of the state governments by ways and means advances. If the limit of W & M exceeds it is called OD. Its interest rate is zero up to 7 days, and it is 3% + bank rate for above seven days.

3. Bankers' Bank

Reserve Bank of India acts as a Bankers' bank for Indian commercial banks when they approach for funds. Because of excessive lending or to conform to the lending requirements of the central government and the RBI, the commercial banks may face liquidity problem. Sometimes to achieve the targets of the planned economy, priority lending and infrastructure funding, these banks may face the shortage of funds. In such circumstances the RBI will act as banker to the commercial banks.

4. Supervising Authority

The RBI acts as a supervising authority in the following ways:

1. To issue licences for the establishment of new banks. The RBI has the power to issue permission to establish new banks after fulfilling all the requirements, like paid up capital, number of directors, necessity of opening bank etc.
2. To issue licences for setting up branches. If the existing bank wants to open its branch in a particular place it has to get permission from the RBI.
3. To prescribe SLR, CRR, Paid up capital, Capital Adequacy Ratio, Statutory Reserves. The RBI has the power to prescribe necessary guidelines and formulate policy to regulate and monitor the activities of banks to maintain safety, liquidity in banks and to safeguard the interests of shareholders, deposits, investors etc.
4. To issue guidelines for working of banks. The RBI with the guidance of MOF will issue guidelines for the working of banks.
5. To conduct investigations. The central bank of a country will have every right to conduct investigations in the

functioning of banks, the portfolio investment, frauds, audit etc. for better supervision.

6. To direct portfolio management of assets. The RBI will issue guidelines for the portfolio investment of assets, like minimum investment on government securities and other securities in the form of SLR. CRR, investment on shares, priority lending, commercial lending, housing etc.
7. To direct portfolio management of investments. Even in the case of investment of the banks RBI will give guidelines to invest on the government and other securities, shares, gold, silver, bullion etc.
8. To approve or force amalgamation. The RBI has the power to direct the banks to go for amalgamation and also approve the amalgamation. (When Global Trust Bank was in trouble it directed the Oriental Bank of Commerce to merge the GTB in 2005.)
9. To evaluate on CAMEL method. The RBI will evaluate the banks on the basis of CAMEL method to see whether these banks have implemented the guidelines issued by it. Here CAMEL stands for:

   C = Capital Adequacy Ratio
   A = Assets Ratios
   M = Management Ratios
   E = Earning Ratios and
   L = Liquidity Ratios

5. Exchange Control Authority

One of the essential functions of the RBI is to maintain the stability of the external value of the rupee. It administers the foreign exchange control through FEMA. It also chooses the exchange rate system and fixes or manages the exchange rate between the rupee and other currencies. It manages exchange reserves and interacts or negotiates with the monetary authorities of the Sterling Area, Asian Clearing Union, and other countries and with international financial institutions.

6. Promoter of the Financial System

The RBI acts as a promoter of financial system. The financial system of a country consists of financial institutions, financial markets, financial instruments and financial services. The RBI is responsible for the promotion of this financial system. The RBI issues guidelines for monitoring the entire financial system by establishing various regulatory authorities through the support of Government of India.

OBJECTIVES OF THE MONETARY POLICY

1. Price stability
2. Controlled expansion of bank credit
3. Promotion of fixed investment
4. Restriction of inventories
5. Promotion of exports and food procurement operations
6. Desired distribution of credit
7. Equitable distribution of credit
8. To promote efficiency in the operations of the financial system
9. Reducing the rigidities

The objectives of the monetary policy of the RBI

1. **Price stability.** To accelerate the economic development in an environment of reasonable price stability, and to develop appropriate institutional set-up to aid this process.
2. **Controlled expansion of bank credit.** The keynote of monetary policy may be put as controlled expansion of bank credit and money supply, with special attention to seasonal requirements for credit without affecting the output in the light of price variations i.e., disinflation without deflation.
3. **Promotion of fixed investment.** The aim of this policy is to restrain non-essential fixed investment and to increase the productivity of investment.
4. **Restriction of inventories.** This policy aims at reducing the inventory to avoid over-stocking, to avoid idle money in

the organizations, becoming sick by overfilling of the stock and also the products produced becoming obsolete.

5. **Promotion of exports and food procurement operations.** It is an independent objective of our monetary policy; special emphasis has been placed to boost the level of exports.
6. **Desired distribution of credit.** It is clearly defined in terms of percentage of credit to be disbursed to priority sectors and small borrowers.
7. **Equitable distribution of credit.** The Reserve Bank always aims equitable distribution to all sectors of the economy and to all social and economic class of people.
8. **To promote efficiency** in the operations of the financial system and to effect appropriate structural changes such as deregulating interest rates, ease operational constraints in the credit delivery system, to introduce new money market instruments, and so on.
9. **Reducing the rigidities**, introducing flexibility, encouraging diversification, promoting more competitive environment, and imparting greater discipline and prudence in the operations of the financial system.

TECHNIQUES OF MONETARY CONTROL OR MONETARY POLICY OF RBI

Monetary policy refers to the policy which aims to maintain low and stable inflation. The sustainable growth of economy depends on maintaining price stability. The price stability is directly related to demand and supply of money in an economy. The techniques of monetary policy adopted by Reserve Bank of India is to control the supply and demand for money in an economy. The increase in supply of money in an economy leads to inflation; the decrease in supply of money will retard the progress of an economy with lack of funds expansion. The increase in demand for money in an economy is an indicator of progress in an economy with good opportunities for investments in various sectors. But it should be properly monitored and channelized for economic development. Similarly decrease in the demand for money shows the lack of investment activities in an economy. For the economic development of country both the supply of money and demand for money should be properly managed by the Ministry of Finance and the Reserve Bank of India. The policy used by the RBI to control the supply and demand for money in an economy is called monetary policy. RBI uses the following techniques of monetary policy.

1. Open Market Operations
2. Bank Rate Policy
3. Discretionary Control of Refinance and Rediscounting
4. Direct Regulation of Interest Rates on Commercial Banks' Deposits and Loans.
5. Cash Reserve Ratio
6. Statutory Reserve Ratio
7. Direct Credit Allocation and Credit Rationing
8. Selective Credit Controls
9. Credit Authorization Scheme
10. Fixation of inventory and Credit Norms
11. Credit Planning
12. Moral Suasion.

1. Open Market Operations (OMOs)

It is a mechanism through which the RBI will regulate the supply of money in the economy by buying and selling of government securities. The RBI will buy the government securities from the market when the supply of money is less through which it injects money into the economy. By this the investment and productive activities in the economy will increase. If the money supply in the economy is more naturally there will be inflation, this also paralyses the growth of the economy hence the RBI, will use the weapon of OMOs and sells government securities in the market. So the money in the economy is withdrawn by the RBI through this mechanism and reduces the inflation rate. The RBI can affect the reserve position of banks, yields on government securities and volume and cost of bank credit. Technically, RBI can conduct OMOs in treasury bills, state government securities, and central government securities: but, in practice, they are conducted only in government securities of all maturities.

The objectives of OMOs are:

a) To control the amount of and changes in bank credit and monetary supply through controlling the reserve base of banks.
b) To make bank rate policy more effective.
c) To maintain stability in government securities market.
d) To support government borrowing programme,
e) To smoothen the seasonal flow of funds in the bank credit market.

2. Bank Rate Policy

The RBI provides financial accommodation in the form of rediscounting of bills of exchange and promissory notes, and loans and advances to scheduled commercial and co-operative banks, SFCs, IDBI, IFC, EXIM Bank, and other approved financial institutions for financing bona fide internal and external commercial trade and production transactions. Section 49 of the RBI Act, 1934 defines it as the standard rate at which the bank is prepared to buy or rediscount bills of exchange or other eligible commercial papers.

This is another technique used by the RBI to monitor the supply and demand for money in an economy. It is used even after the economic reforms. The present bank rate is 6 percent. It is basis for determining the interest rates of the financial institutions.

3. Variable Reserve Requirements

Commercial banks in India, as in many other countries in the world, are subject to a host of control measures of the Central Bank, apart from the selective control of credit exercised by the Reserve Bank of India. It controls the volume of credit in a quantitative way so as to influence the total volume of credit.

The commercial banks in India are required to keep a certain percentage of deposits as reserves with the Reserve Bank. The Reserve Bank is legally authorized to raise or lower the minimum reserves that the bank must maintain against the total deposits. If the percentage of reserves to be maintained is increased, the commercial banks will be left with less cash and if the percentage of reserves to be maintained is decreased the commercial banks will have more cash with them and they would be able to expand credit. The Statutory Liquidity Reserve for banks is one of the tools of monetary control in the hands of the Reserve Bank. There are two distinct ways in which the SLR operates as an instrument of monetary control: one is by affecting the borrowings of the government from the RBI; the other is by controling the freedom of banks to sell government securities or borrow against them from the RBI. In both the ways the creation of high-powered money, and thereby variations in the supply of money is affected.

Under the statutory liquidity requirements, each bank is required to maintain a prescribed minimum proportion of its daily total demand and time liabilities in the form of designated liquid assets. These liquid assets consist of excess reserves, unencumbered government and other approved securities and current account balances with other banks.

Excess reserves are defined as total reserves minus statutory or required reserves with the RBI. Securities are unencumbered if loans have not been taken against them from the RBI. Investments in government securities are securities in central and state government securities, including treasury bills, treasury deposit receipts, treasury savings deposit certificates, and postal obligation such as National Plan Certificates, NSCs etc. other approved securities are securities of state associated bodies.

4. Cash Reserve Ratio

According to RBI Act of 1934, Scheduled Commercial banks were required to keep minimum cash reserves of five per cent of their demand liabilities and two per cent of their time liabilities with the Reserve Bank. The amendment Act of 1956 empowered the Reserve Bank to use these reserve requirements as a weapon of credit control by varying them between five and twenty per cent on the demand liabilities. In September 1962, the Act was further amended, with the amendment the distinction between the demand and time liabilities for the purpose of reserve requirements vanished and statutorily the reserve requirements were fixed uniformly at three per cent of the banks' total demand and time liabilities (DTL) in India. Moreover, the Reserve Bank was empowered to vary the minimum CRR between three per cent and fifteen per cent (the maximum not to exceed 15 per cent at any time) and this variability in cash reserves ratio directly affects the availability and cost of credit. An increase in CRR leads to immediate curb on the excess funds of the banks, then banks' credit volume decreases, their profit also decreases. To maintain the same total profit, a decrease in profitability is to be compensated by raising the lending rate. Eventually, when the bank's lending rates are raised, the cost of credit increases.

During busy seasons as well as in normal periods of a growing economy, demand for credit by the banks' customers usually tends to be high and/or raising. Then, often banks have to borrow from the Reserve Bank, which is a lender of last resort. In the process, during the inflationary period when the Reserve Bank liberally functions as the lender of last resort, it acts contrary to its own intention by impounding banks' liquidity by raising CRR. The RBI's reliance on CRR as a primary weapon of monetary control on account of the large extent of monetization of public debt in supporting the Government deficits is increasing its scope in recent years.

On the side of the policy actions emanating from the Committee on Financial Sector Reforms (CFS) recommendations, there has already been progressive and significant reduction of the SLR and the CRR to the current levels of 25 percent and 5 percent from 38 per cent and 15 percent on NDTL in 1991 respectively. As part of rationalization measures, effective from

October 25, 1997, interest paid by the Reserve Bank on eligible cash balances maintained under CRR of banks was raised to 4 per cent per annum on eligible cash balances over the minimum 3 per cent of CRR.

5. Discretionary Control of Refinance and Rediscounting

This technique is used to regulate the cost and availability of refinance, and to change the volume of lendable resources of banks and other financial institutions.

6. Direct Credit Allocation and Credit Rationing

The weakening of the bank rate and direct administration of interest rates in the economy necessitated the use of complex system of quantitative credit controls or credit ceiling. The distribution or allocation of credit among different sectors, borrowers, and users was increasingly achieved through the fixation of specific and direct quantitative credit ceilings or credit targets. A few examples of ceilings are non-food credit, priority sector lending, agricultural sector advances, advances to rural artisans, village craftsmen and cottage industries.

7. The Selective Credit Controls

The seasonal nature of the Indian economy and the nature of inflation necessitated the Selective Credit Controls. The SCCs seek to change the composition of credit. They are used to reduce the supply of credit in certain directions and to encourage it in desired directions. They have been used to prevent speculative hoarding in speculative commodities such as paddy, rice, wheat, pulses, oil-seeds, oils and vanaspati, cotton, sugar, gur and so on. They are also applied to unsecured or clean credit by banks, and credit given for trading in shares. RBI used SCCs normally in three forms: 1. Fixation of margin requirements, 2. Fixation of separated minimum lending rates on credit covered by SCCs, and 3. Fixation of ceiling on *ex ante* flows of credit.

8. Credit Authorization Scheme

This scheme was launched in the year 1965. The credit authorization scheme is a scheme of RBI, through its monetary policy which authorizes the commercial banks and other financial institutions to give credit to the desired sectors as per its guidelines. The guidelines are framed by the RBI with an objective of achieving the goals of a desired economy.

The objectives of this scheme are:

a) To regulate credit to control inflation.
b) To enforce financial discipline on large borrowers.
c) To ensure that end-use of credit is for genuine productive purposes.
d) To ensure that large borrowers do not pre-empt or monopolize scarce bank credit and
e) To ensure that credit is supplied in accordance with the needs of borrowers and the goals of planning.

9. Fixation of Inventory and Credit Norms

The studies revealed that certain striking features of the banking system which needed to be reformed. It was discovered that banks tended to sanction excessive credit limits or over finance industrial units. There was gross inter-utilisation of credit limits sanctioned. The banks' credit limits tended to exceed their total deposits. Hence there was an over-reliance and over-accumulation on cash credit system while bill finance was not very popular. Payments period in respect of trade credit of industrial units tended to be long or extended.

10. Credit Planning

This was launched by the RBI during the year 1967-68. It was a product of the environment of economic planning. Its objectives are:

a) To regulate the expansion in the overall quantum of funds to a desired level, and

b) To direct flows of funds to desired sectors, areas, purposes, uses, so that the objectives of monetary policy are achieved. In other words, the quantum and distribution (allocation) of credit in qualitative and directional aspects were envisaged, regulated and monitored through credit planning.

11. Moral Suasion

It takes the form of writing letters and holding discussions between the RBI and the banks about trends in the economy in general and in money, credit and finance in particular, and about the measures which ought to be taken from time to time in the light of national objectives.

NATIONAL BANK FOR AGRICULTURE AND RURAL DEVELOPMENT (NABARD)

NABARD is an apex institution, accredited with all matters concerning policy, planning and operations in the field of credit for agriculture and other economic activities in rural areas in India. The Committee to Review Arrangements for Institutional Credit for Agriculture and Rural Development (CRAFICARD), constituted by the Reserve Bank of India (RBI) under the Chairmanship of Shri B. Sivaraman, conceived and recommended the establishment of the National Bank for Agriculture and Rural Development (NABARD). The Indian Parliament through the Act 61 of 1981 approved the setting up of NABARD. The Bank came into existence on 12 July, 1982 and was dedicated to the service of the nation by the Hon'ble Prime Minister, Smt. Indira Gandhi on 5 November, 1982.

Initiatives taken to establish and to develop an agency to cater to agricultural sector till the establishment of NABARD

- Reserve Bank of India (RBI) established in 1935 inter alia, with a mandate to set up a special Agricultural Credit Department (ACD) with expert staff.

- Agricultural Refinance Corporation (ARC) was established in 1963 to support investment credit needs for agricultural development.
- Consequent to undertaking of development and promotional functions, ARC was renamed as Agricultural Refinance and Development Corporation (ARDC) in 1972.
- RBI, at the instance of Government of India (GOI) appointed a Committee to Review Arrangements for Institutional Credit for Agriculture and Rural Development (CRAFICARD) in 1979.
- The CRAFICARD recommended the establishment of National Bank for Agriculture and Rural Development (NABARD).
- National Bank for Agriculture and Rural Development Act, 1981 was passed by the Indian Parliament and NABARD was established on 12 July 1982 with an initial capital of Rs. 100 crores. The capital is enhanced to Rs. 2000 crores subscribed by the Government of India and Reserve Bank of India.

NABARD is established as a development bank, in terms of the Preamble of the Act, "for providing and regulating credit and other facilities for the promotion and development of agriculture, small scale industries, cottage and village industries, handicrafts and other rural crafts and other allied economic activities in rural areas with a view to promoting integrated rural development and securing prosperity of rural areas and for matters connected therewith or incidental thereto."

NABARD took over the functions of the erstwhile Agricultural Credit Department (ACD) and Rural Planning and Credit Cell (RPCC) of RBI and Agricultural Refinance and Development Corporation (ARDC). It is subscribed and paid-up capital was Rs. 100 crores which was enhanced to Rs. 500 crores, contributed by the Government of India (GOI) and RBI in equal proportions. Currently it is Rs. 2000 crores, contributed by the GOI (Rs.550 crores) and the RBI (Rs.1450 crores).

Objectives of NABARD

NABARD is an apex institution in India which provides help for agriculture and rural development. It has been established with the following purposes.

1. To give undivided attention and purposeful direction to integrated rural development.
2. To act as a centrepiece for the entire rural credit system at the national level.
3. To act as a provider of supplemental funding to rural credit institutions.
4. To arrange for investment credit to small industries, village and cottage industries, handicrafts and other rural crafts, artisans, and farmers.
5. To improve the credit distribution system by institution building, rehabilitation of credit institutions and training of bank personnel.
6. To provide refinance facilities to SLDBs, SCBs, RRBs, and commercial banks for development purposes in rural areas.
7. To coordinate the working of different agencies engaged in the deployment works in rural areas.
8. To inspect, monitor and evaluate projects getting refinance from the NABARD.

Functions of NABARD

The functions of NABARD have been divided into three categories. They are:

1. Credit distribution function.
2. Developmental functions and
3. Regulatory functions.

1. Credit distribution function

The NABARD provides refinance of various types to the ***short term credit*** institutions like State Cooperative Boards (SCBs), Regional Rural Banks (RRBs) and other financial institutions approved by the RBI for the following purposes. Seasonal agricultural operations, marketing of agricultural produce, marketing and distribution of inputs like pesticides, fertilizers, hybrid seeds etc. production and marketing of handicrafts, artisans' products of village and cottage industries etc.

Medium term credit to SCBs, Land Development Banks (LDBs), RRBs, and other approved institutions for a period ranging from 18 months to 7 years. These term loans are given for investment schemes relating to agriculture and rural sector.

Long term credit to State Land Development Banks, RRBs, commercial banks, SCBs, and to any approved financial institution. It provides refinance for investment in the the activities like minor irrigation, land development, soil conservation, dairy development poultry farming fish farming, storage and market yard, silk production biogas and other alternative sources of energy projects in the villages. The duration of loans is for a period of 25 years.

It provides ***refinance facilities*** to SCBs and RRBs in the event of changes and rearrangement of credits when there are calamities like drought, famine, war, earthquakes etc. The duration of these refinance facilities is for a period not more than 7 years. NABRD provides ***refinancing facilities to all small, village and cottage industries*** in rural areas.

2. Developmental functions

NABARD performs the following developmental function:

1. Co-coordinating rural credit institutions.
2. Improving the capacity of credit delivery system.
3. Solving the problems of agriculture and villages by developing specialized institutions.
4. To help the government, RBI, and other institutions in their rural development efforts.
5. To provide facilities for research and training to the staff of RRBs, SCBs, LDBs etc.

3. Regulatory functions

It performs the following regulatory functions.

1. It inspects the working of RRBs and cooperative banks of all types except the primary cooperative banks.
2. In inspects apex cooperative marketing federations. State handloom weaving societies, which are financed on voluntary basis.
3. All applications for opening of a branch by the RRB or a cooperative bank and other primary cooperative society are required to submit to the RBI through NABARD.
4. All RRBs and cooperative banks submitting returns to the RBI are required to submit a copy of returns to the NABARD also.
5. It has the power to obtain any information from the RRBs and cooperative banks if necessary.

Organization of NABARD

It is managed by a 15 member Board of Directors consisting of Chairman, Managing Director, two expert of rural economists, three experts from cooperative and commercial banks, three directors from the current directors of the RBI, three directors from the GOI, and two directors representing the state governments.

NABARD operates throughout the country through its 28 regional offices and one sub-office, located in the capitals of all the states/union territories. It has 336 district offices across the country, one sub-office at Port Blair and one special cell at Srinagar. It also has 6 training establishments.

Major Activities of NABARD

The major activities of NABARD are:

1. ***Production Credit***. NABARD provides short-term refinance for various types of production/marketing/ procurement activities like seasonal agricultural operations which are in the process of raising various crops and are seasonally recurring in nature, financing of weavers, financing of other seasonal agricultural operations,

refinancing for marketing of crops, for procurement, stocking and distribution of chemical fertilizers etc.

2. ***Investment Credit***. NABARD provides investment credit in the form of medium-term and long-term refinancing assistance to institutions and agencies that are engaged in agricultural financing activities.
3. **Minor Irrigation**. Water is the most essential single input required for increasing the agricultural productivity. The investments eligible for NABARD Refinance under the minor irrigation development are groundwater schemes, shallow and deep tubewells, borewells, filter points etc.
4. **Plantation and Horticulture**. It covers development of some specified fruit crops, plantation crops, medicinal plants, essential oils, vegetable crops and others.
5. **Land Development, Soil Conservation and Water Management.** Judicious use of land and water resources, soil health improvement and reclamation of degraded lands are prerequisites for increasing agricultural production.
6. **Animal Husbandry**. The refinance assistance for animal husbandry activities is provided by NABARD.
7. **Development of Fisheries Sector.** Some of the activities like marine fisheries, inland fisheries, and ancillary activities like ice plants and cold storage, processing and value addition activities, feed mill, net making units are eligible for development under NABARD.
8. **Research and development activities.** NABARD extends its refinancing assistance to enable firms to undertake research and developmental activities.

THE SECURITIES AND EXCHANGE BOARD OF INDIA (SEBI)

Post-liberalization era in India brought many changes in the Indian financial system. The Indian financial system witnessed an unprecedented growth in terms of the number and the variety of players like foreign institutional investors, domestic institutional investors like mutual funds, pension funds, insurance companies, and so on. The number of active investors, institutions and intermediaries increased manifold. The stock exchanges also grew in number to 22 in addition to Over the Counter Exchange (OTCE). The functioning of the stock exchanges in India has the following weaknesses.

1. Long delays in settlements
2. Lack of transparency in procedures.
3. Vulnerable to price rigging,
4. Insider trading.

All these factors necessitated the need for creating an awareness and interest among common investors. The growth of corporate enterprises ushered in excellent investment opportunities available in the securities market among the lay savers.

The need for setting up a statutory apex body was felt by the government to promote an orderly and healthy growth of the securities market and for investor protection. The government of India set up the Securities and Exchange Board of India on April 12, 1988 on the recommendations of a high powered committee on Stock Exchange Reforms headed by G. S. Patel, The SEBI got its legal status by the Securities and Exchange Board of India Ordinance, in 1992, which is located in Bombay. The members of the Board of Management of the SEBI comprised those drawn from professional brokers, financial consultants, merchant bankers, investors, stock exchange authorities, finance ministry, etc.

Constitution and Organization

The body of SEBI consists of a Chairman, two members from amongst the officials of the ministries of the central government dealing with finance and law, one member from amongst the officials of the RBI and two members to be appointed by the central government. The general superintendence, direction and management of the affairs of the Board shall vest in a Board member, which may exercise all powers and do all acts and things which may be exercised or done by the Board.

Objectives of SEBI

SEBI was set up with the objectives of assisting and facilitating the mobilization of adequate resources through the securities market and its efficient allocation, keeping in mind the interests of issuers, investors and the intermediaries.

The objective of SEBI Act is "to protect the interests of investors in securities and to promote the development of and regulate the securities market and also for matters connected therewith or incidental thereto".

The objectives of SEBI are:

1. To help and create an atmosphere for raising money from the capital market.
2. To gain the confidence and trust of investors, particularly the small and general investor.
3. To co-ordinate and connect the process involved in corporate-investment, so that the benefit of investments can be passed on to the interested investors only.
4. Educating and creating awareness among investors of corporate sector by providing all the information needed for wise investment.
5. To create proper investment climate and enable the corporate sector to raise industrial securities easily, efficiently and at reasonable cost.
6. To help and build the infrastructure needed to encourage capital market in the country.
7. To regularise the services by recognizing the routine procedures followed in completing a transaction by middlemen like brokers, commercial banks, merchant banks etc.
8. To ensure unprejudiced atmosphere for mergers and take-over by companies ensuring fair and equal treatment to all the security holders.

9. To create an orderly and more open atmosphere for investors from outside the country.

Powers and Functions of SEBI

The important functions of SEBI are:

1. Regulating the business in stock exchanges and any other securities markets.
2. Registering and regulating the working of stock brokers, sub-brokers, share transfer agents, bankers to issue, trustees of trust deeds, registrar to issue, merchant bankers, underwriters, portfolio managers, and other intermediaries.
3. Registering and regulating the working of depositories, participants, custodian of securities, foreign institutional investors, credit rating agencies etc.
4. Registering and regulating the working of collective investment schemes, including mutual funds.
5. Promoting and regulating self-regulatory organizations.
6. Prohibiting fraudulent and unfair trade practices relating to securities markets.
7. Promoting investor's education and training of intermediaries of securities markets.
8. Prohibiting insider trading in securities, with the imposition of monetary penalties on erring market intermediaries.
9. Regulating substantial acquisition of shares and takeover of companies.
10. Calling for information from, carrying out inspection, conducting inquiries and audits of the stock exchanges and intermediaries and self-regulatory organizations in the securities market.

EXERCISE

Two marks questions

1. Mention the organization structure of RBI.
2. What does the CAMEL represent?

3. What do you mean by CRR? What is the present ratio of CRR?
4. What do you mean by SLR? What is its percentage today in India?
5. What do you mean OPMs?
6. What is bank rate policy?
7. What is meant by moral suasion?
8. What do you mean by monetary policy?
9. Mention two objectives of credit planning.
10. Why NABARD was established?
11. How NABARD is organized?
12. Why SEBI was established? Explain the functions of SEBI.

Five marks questions

1. What are the supervisory authorities of RBI?
2. What is OMOs? Mention its objectives.
3. Explain the variable reserve ratio.
4. What do you mean by credit authorization scheme? What are its objectives?
5. What are the purposes of establishing NABARD?
6. Mention important activities of NABARD.

Fifteen marks questions

1. Explain the role of Reserve Bank of India.
2. What are the functions of RBI? Explain.
3. What is meant by monetary policy? Explain its objectives.
4. Explain the relevance of monetary policy of RBI in an economy.
5. Critically evaluate the techniques of monetary policy.
6. Explain the functions of NABARD.

Skill Development

1. Collect a copy of recent monetary policy announced by RBI and observe the changes effected in the banking sector.

Chapter 5
BANKING INNOVATIONS

OUTLINE

- Goals of E-Banking
- Advantages of Computerization in Banks
- New Technology in Banking
- Banking Technology: A Brief Perspective
- Electronic Fund Transfer
- Automated Teller Machines
- Debit Cards
- Credit Cards
- Smart Cards
- Magnetic Ink Character Recognition
- Virtual Banking

LEARNING OBJECTIVES

After studying this chapter you should be able to answer:

1. What is meant by e-banking?
2. What are the goals of e-banking?
3. Advantages of computerization.
4. What are the e-banking services?
5. What are the benefits of each e-banking service?

GOALS OF E-BANKING

The use of Information Technology has become inevitable with the development of banking and financial system in India and the integration of international financial markets with computerization. The Reserve Bank of India appointed a committee on computerization in 1983, which submitted its report in 1984. The RBI in 1988 constituted the second Rangarajan Committee to draw up a perspective plan for computerization in banks and to suggest modalities for implementing on-line computerization. The committee submitted its report in 1989 and the computerization settlement of October 1993 was signed between the IBA and the bank employees' unions to reduce the resistance from labour unions for computerization as suggested by the Rangarajan Committee.

In the 1990s, the banking sector in India saw greater emphasis being placed on technology and innovation. Banks began to use technology to provide better quality of services at greater speed. Internet banking and mobile banking made it convenient for customers to do their banking from geographically diverse places. Banks also sharpened their focus on rural markets and introduced a variety of services geared to the special needs of their rural customers. Banking activities also transcended their traditional scope and new concepts like personal banking, retailing and bank assurance were introduced. The sector was also moving rapidly towards universal banking and electronic transactions, which were expected to change the way banking would be perceived in the future.

Banking has become a highly competitive business, the business of risk taking and risk management, developing customer base, speed and accuracy are vitally important in banking. For these reasons, IT in banking becomes inevitable. Electronic banking refers to doing banking business by using electronic devices like computer, internet and networking, MICR, EFT, and so on to increase efficiency, quick service, productivity and transparency in its transactions.

The specific goals of the electronic banking are:

1. To achieve transparency and accountability
2. To establish frame for continuous quality improvement
3. Using the available technology and tools for increasing productivity and reduction in costs
4. To achieve uniformity of records, verifiability and micro level monitoring

5. Building customer interface
6. Better management of bank's funds and risks
7. Reducing transaction costs.

ADVANTAGES OF COMPUTERIZATION IN BANKS

There are many advantages of computerization.

1. Large data is stored for information and better decision making is easy.
2. Accuracy of information is considerably improved and the quality of the decisions improves.
3. Problems are handled more easily by using various operation research models.
4. The cost involved in the decision making process is reduced.
5. Lots of information is stored for future reference.
6. Paper work is reduced to the minimum.
7. It enables instant preparation of reports and facilitates easy processing of complex calculations. It ensures better customer service through quick access to data and processing.
8. More secrecy can be maintained.
9. A customer can avail service in any branch from anywhere.
10. Customer can have information about his account, transfer funds from one bank to another bank even at comfort of staying at home.

Paper-based *versus* Electronic Transactions

Year	Volume (in million)			Value (Rs. crore)		
	Paper-based	Electronic	Total	Paper-based	Electronic	Total
1	2	3	4	5	6	7
2002-03	1,014	173	1,187	1,34,24,313	37,536	1,34,61,849
2003-04	1,023	224	1,247	1,15,94,976	67,352	1,16,62,328
2004-05	1,125	432	1,557	1,10,47,052	42,24,746	1,52,71,798

Paper-based versus Electronic Transactions-Relative Flows (Value)

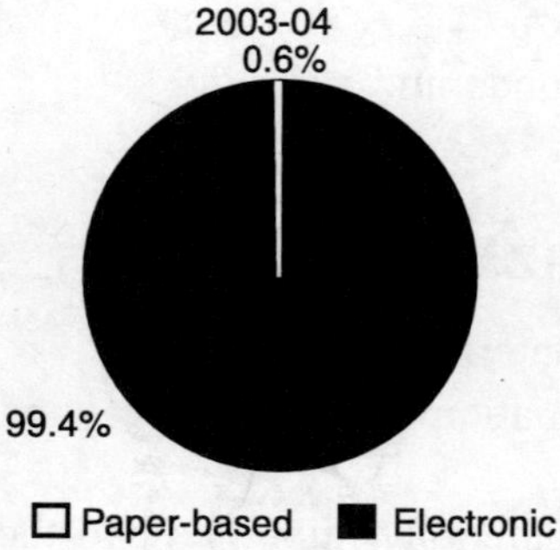

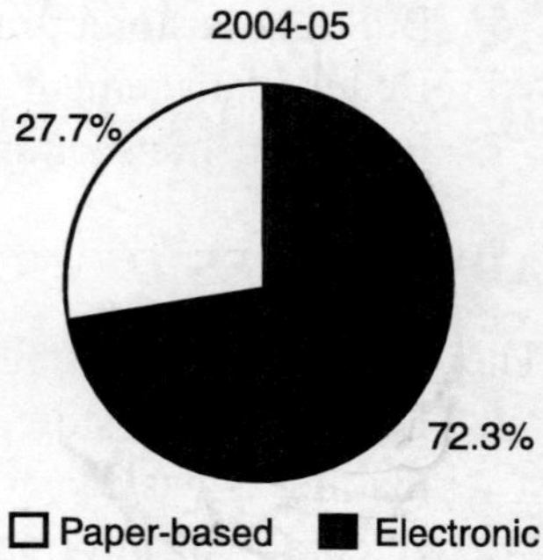

As a result of sharp increase in RTGS and other electronic transactions, the proportion of electronic transactions both in volume and value terms has increased sharply. Electronic payments are cheaper as they have lower production cost than paper-based instruments. They can also be carried out faster in comparison with paper-based transactions. The increased use of electronic payments has thus increased the efficiency of the payment system.

NEW TECHNOLOGY IN BANKING

In banking industry the role of technology is playing a vital role. The success of the bank now mainly depends upon the using of technology. This is because of increase in the competition in rendering services, awareness among consumers, expectations of consumers and availability of technology. The following are the hi-tech banking technology services in the Indian banking industry.

- Shared Payment Network System (SPANS)
- Automated Clearing House Operations
- E-banking
- Electronic Funds Transfer (EFT)
- Electronic Clearing Service (ECS) – credit clearing and debit clearing

- Computerized Message Transfer (COMET)
- Very Small Aperture Terminal (VSAT)
- Smart Cards
- Debit and credit cards
- Internet Banking
- ATM
- Magnetic Ink Character Recognizer (MICR)
- Virtual /Digital/e-sign Signatures in Banking
- Society for Worldwide inter-bank Financial Telecommunication (SWIFT) etc.

BANKING TECHNOLOGY: A BRIEF PERSPECTIVE

E-Banking

It is a generic name for the range of technology that allows the exchange of information electronically related to banking transactions. An account holder with internet banking facility is given a password. He can use Internet banking for services such as viewing operation of an account, credit card, home loan balance, e-mail queries, feedback form, order chequebooks, stop payment of a cheque, accrued interest, fees and taxes, pay bills, transfer funds to the other pay accounts etc.

The various components of e-banking are:

1) Internet/intranet/extranet
2) Electronic data interchange
3) E-mail
4) Electronic Fund Transfer
5) Smart Card.

Internet Banking

The internet banking is an extremely comprehensive product for both retail and corporate use. It has acquired real-time transaction processing capability and has been supporting the business initiatives of the bank in the areas of bill payments, IR application money receipts, credit card payments, insurance premium payments; access the account from personal computers, transfer of funds from one bank to another bank etc.

Internet banking involves use of the internet for delivery of banking products and services. It allows customers to transact business online and in real time. There are different levels in internet banking. Some banks offer only the most basic services, such as access to deposit account data, requisition of cheque books, etc., on the internet, while others offer an entire gamut of services, like investment advice and sales of additional products like insurance and mutual funds. Internet banking is a broad field and covers technology options like ATMs, banking kiosks, mobile banking etc.

ELECTRONIC FUND TRANSFER (EFT)

EFT will help the banks to improve customer service and reducing the cost of drafts and mail transfer. The electronic credit clearing service enables direct credit of the dividends to the shareholders accounts without the use of paper instruments. The advantages of EFT are:

1. Avoiding of printing MICR cheques.
2. Avoiding postal delays.
3. Avoiding postage.
4. Avoiding reconciliation problems.
5. Avoiding loss of instruments.
6. Avoiding fraud and burden on the clearing system.

AUTOMATED TELLER MACHINES (ATMs)

ATM stands for Automated Teller Machine. First ATM was installed in London by Barclays Bank in 1967. In India HSBC was the first bank to install ATM in the year 1987. ATM is a computerized machine used for paying/withdrawing money, statement inquiries, stop payment instructions, requisition for cheque books/drafts, bill payments and transfer of funds. It is operated by a magnetic plastic card and Personal Identification Number (PIN). ATMs are the most dynamic retail channel today in terms of the transformation. They are bringing about radical changes in banking habits and their popularity with branch customers and the staff is evident.

ATMs can be on-line and off-line. On-line ATMs are connected to the server facilitating real time access and they are attached to branches while in case of off-line ATMS the withdrawals are integrated with the server after a lapse of time, and they are located away from the branches e.g., market places.

Functions Performed by ATM

ATMs perform the following functions in banks:

1. It can perform both cash and non-cash transaction in a totally secured environment.
2. It helps to perform cash transactions for both deposits and withdrawals.

DEBIT CARDS

It is an electronic card one can use as a convenient payment mechanism. The card is generally issued by the bank and is connected through the ATM. Debit cards allow the holder to spend only what is in his account and purchases should be kept track of just like a writing cheque book. A debit card is basically better way of carrying cash or a cheque book.

Definition: Debit cards are similar to credit cards, except debit cards pull money out of your account. Debit cards do *not* create or increase a loan like credit cards do.

There are two types of debit cards:

1. Direct Debit Card
2. Deferred Debit card

1. **Direct Debit Card**: It allows only on-line transactions. It is also called point-of-sale. It is an immediate electronic transfer of money from your bank account to the merchant's (vendors) account. It helps the customer then and there to find the credit balance in the account.
2. **Deferred Debit Card**: It looks similar to a credit card, bearing a Visa or Master Card logo, and used wherever

the card's brand name is displayed. This card allows off-line transactions, as well as on-line. The off-line purchases resemble a credit card transaction. In this case merchant's terminal reads the card and creates a debit against the individual's account within two or three days but not immediately.

Uses of Debit Card

1. Availing debit card is easy because the account holder after opening his bank account will be qualified for getting the debit card facility if this facility is there in the bank.
2. The user of the card during making transaction need not show any identification card or personal information.
3. The debit card will free you from carrying cash or a cheque book.
4. For international travellers, it can save from having a stock of traveller's cheques or cash during their travel.
5. Debit cards are readily accepted than cheques.
6. The payment of penalty doesn't arise in the case of debit card since the question of delayed payment never comes.
7. The debit card can be used to make smaller value payments, avoiding the need to withdraw cash form the bank for such petty expenses.

CREDIT CARDS

Credit cards are an easy method to buy now and pay later. A credit card is a mechanism which enables card holders to purchase goods and services without paying immediately. The holders can use the cards to get credit from banks up to certain limit both cash withdrawal and credit payments for 45 days without interest. Later the customer can pay entire amount or opt for revolving credit system for up to 2.95 percent of interest per month. The credit card system relieves the botheration of carrying cash and ensures safety. It is a convenience of extended credit without formality.

SMART CARDS

Smart cards are like credit cards, with an implanted computer chip on them. This computer chip will store the sensitive data and processes them. The smart cards are of three types. The storage/memory cards, intelligent cards and the hybrid cards. The smart cards will work like this. The smart card has to be inserted into a smart card reader, which in turn reads the information stored on the card. Then the reader can update the information on the card. The smart card has a built in security keys like Personal Identification Number. This PIN will authenticate the user. Tampering with a smart card is difficult since this would destroy the microchip inside it. It is an intrinsically secure device.

Although cash continues to be used heavily in retail transactions in India, the use of cheques and several other payment instruments such as credit cards, debit cards and smart cards, on the whole, has been increasing in recent years. The use of payment cards, both in volume and value terms, more than doubled in 2004-05. The use of electronic payments in the form of ECS, EFT and SEFT is also on increase.

Retail Electronic and Card-based Payments

(Value in Rs. crore)

Year	Retail Electronic@		Card-based #		Total	
	Volume	Value	Volume	Value	Volume	Value
2000-01	N.A.	N.A.	N.A.	N.A.	N.A.	N.A.
2001-02	17,770	6,123	N.A.	N.A.	17,770	6,123
2002-03	23,660	10,222	N.A.	N.A.	23,660	10,222
2003-04	29,046	29,933	1,85,501	35,870	2,14,547	65,803
2004-05	57,071	79,479	3,62,040	77,120	4,19,111	2,30,500

N.A. : Not Available.
@ :ECS (Debit and Credit), EFT and SEFT.
# : Credit cards, debit cards and smart cards.
Note : Volume represents number of transactions.

MAGNETIC INK CHARACTER RECOGNITION (MICR)

MICR is an acronym for Magnetic Ink Character Recognition. It is the automation concept used by the banking industry. Every negotiable document, like cheques and money orders, has a unique style of numbers and symbols with magnetic properties.

Negotiable documents like cheques and money orders have a special line of numbers and symbols located on the bottom of the cheque. These characters are printed in a special font with magnetically chargeable toner. Financial institutions and the RBI process negotiable documents with high-speed reader/sorter equipment. These machines give a magnetic charge to the bottom of the cheque and then read the MICR line in three hundredths of a second. Cheques travel through reader/sorters at 20 miles per hour or 2,400 documents per minute. As the "average" cheque travels through the banking system it is read seven times by reader/sorter equipment at many locations. Some cheques are fed through these machines up to 20 times. The high-speed automated processing of negotiable documents depends on the accuracy and the integrity of the MICR line. This helps the banker to clear the cheques of one banker with another banker in that region and the account of the banker is adjusted by debiting and crediting it.

VIRTUAL BANKING

Virtual banking denotes the provision of banking and related services through extensive use of IT without direct recourse to the bank by the customer. The origin of VB in the developed countries can be traced back to the seventies with the installation of ATMs. The principal types of virtual banking services are ATMs, Shared ATM networks, EFT at point of sale, smart cards, store-valve cards, phone banking, internet and intranet banking.

Advantages

The advantages of virtual banking (VB) are:

1. VB has the advantage of having a lower cost of handling a transaction when compared to the cost of handling via the branch.
2. The increased speed of response to customer requirements to increase customer satisfaction.
3. The lower cost of operating branch network along with reduced staff costs leads to cost efficiency.
4. VB allows the possibility of improved quality and an enlarged range of services.

Technological Progress in Banks

Several banks have been positioning themselves as a ***one-stop shop*** financial service provider with a fairly exhaustive range of products, including deposit products, loans, credit cards, debit cards, depository (custody services), investment advice, bill payments and various transactional services. Apart from these, banks have also been entering into the business of selling third-party products such as mutual funds and insurance to the retail customers. To provide their customers greater flexibility and convenience as well as to reduce servicing costs, banks have been investing to computerize their branches and in new delivery channels such as ATMs, phone banking, internet banking and mobile banking.

Computerization in Public Sector Banks (As on March 31, 2005)

	(Per cent)
i) Branches already fully computerised	60.0
ii) Branches under core banking solution	11.0
iii) Fully computerised branches (i + ii)	71.0
Partially computerised branches	21.8

: Other than branches under Core Banking Solution

Source: *Trend and Progress of Banking in India 2005*

Branches and ATMs of Scheduled Commercial Banks

(As at end-March 2005)

Bank Group	Number of Branches	On-site	Off-site	Total Number of ATMs
Nationalised Banks	33,627	3,205	1,567	4,772
State Bank Group	13,661	1,548	3,672	5,220
Old Private Sector Banks	4,511	800	441	1,241
New Private Sector Banks	1,685	1,883	3,729	5,612
Foreign Banks	242	218	579	797

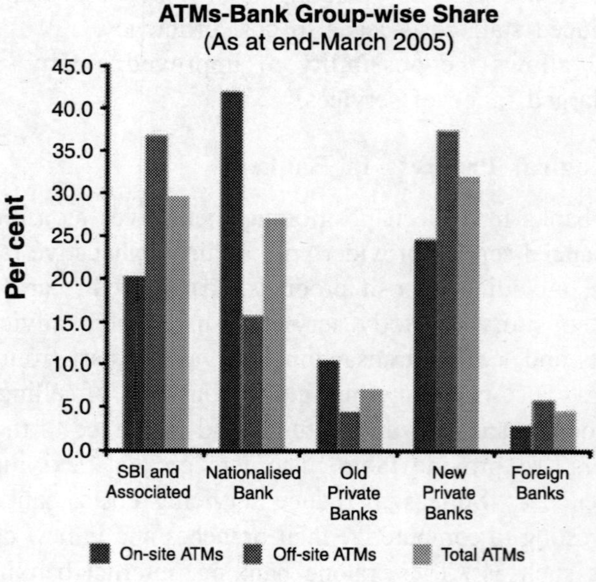

Total number of ATMs installed in the country was 17,642 at end-March 2005. New private sector banks constituted the largest share of ATMs, followed by the SBI group, nationalized banks, old private sector banks and foreign banks. While nationalized banks and old private sector banks had more on-site ATMs than off-site ATMs, SBI group, new private sector banks and foreign banks had more off-site ATMs than on-site ATMs (see Chart). Off-site ATMs as percentage to total branches was the highest in the case of foreign banks, followed by new private sector banks, SBI group, old private sector banks and nationalized banks.

EXERCISE

Two marks questions

1. What is e-banking?
2. What do you mean by Internet Banking?
3. What is EFT?
4. What do you mean by debit cards?
5. What do you mean by credit cards?
6. What do you mean by Smart Card?
7. What do you mean by MICR?
8. Mention the uses of MICR.
9. What is virtual banking?

Five marks questions

1. What is EFT? Mention its advantages.
2. What do you mean by ATMs? Explain its functions.
3. What do you mean by virtual banking? Explain its advantages.

Fifteen marks questions

1. Discuss the role of new technology services in Indian Banking Industry.
2. Evaluate the relevance of IT in banking.
3. Explain the role of debit cards in Indian banking sector.

Skill Development

1. Prepare a model to show how credit card works.
2. Take a cheque leaf and identify the MICR code.
3. Prepare a list of some important foreign currencies and find out the value of these against Indian currency.
4. Give a visit to a nearby bank and interact with the official of the bank to identify the e-services offered by that bank.